THE AWAKENED LIFE

AN 8-WEEK GUIDE TO STUDENT WELL-BEING

SARAH E. BOLLINGER
ANGELA R. OLSEN

HIGHER EDUCATION & MINISTRY
General Board of Higher Education and Ministry

THE UNITED METHODIST CHURCH

The Awakened Life: An 8-Week Guide to Student Well-Being

The General Board of Higher Education and Ministry leads and serves The United Methodist Church in the recruitment, preparation, nurture, education, and support of Christian leaders—lay and clergy—for the work of making disciples of Jesus Christ for the transformation of the world. Its vision is that a new generation of Christian leaders will commit boldly to Jesus Christ and be characterized by intellectual excellence, moral integrity, spiritual courage, and holiness of heart and life. The General Board of Higher Education and Ministry of The United Methodist Church serves as an advocate for the intellectual life of the church. The Board's mission embodies the Wesleyan tradition of commitment to the education of laypersons and ordained persons by providing access to higher education for all persons.

The Awakened Life: An 8-Week Guide to Student Well-Being

All web addresses were correct and operational at the time of publication.

GBHEM Publishing is an affiliate member of the Association of University Presses.

ISBN 978-1-945935-49-7

Manufactured in the United States of America

HIGHER EDUCATION & MINISTRY
General Board of Higher Education and Ministry
THE UNITED METHODIST CHURCH

CONTENTS

The Awakened Life Student Guide

The Awakened Life Leader Guide

PREFACE

Dear Reader,

The simple but profound purpose of this guide is to help you awaken to life. Too many of us live our lives believing anxiety, depression, worry, isolation, and fear are all life has to offer. This guide reveals that there is an alternative way to live. It is an invitation for you to experience the awakened life.

Written through the lens of the Christian faith and using mindfulness as a guiding framework, this guide intentionally invites people of all faiths to join in this journey, as the insights and tools offered can be meaningful to all people. This is not your typical Bible study, nor is it a self-help guide. Instead, this guide is designed to help people awaken to the possibility of experiencing well-being in each moment.

Each person defines well-being differently. We define it as a deep awareness of God that offers us an innate sense of self-worth, a deep connection with others, a profound link to nature, and a forever hope. It is not a someday or after-death kind of health and hope—it is wholeness experienced *now*.

In our own lives of faith, we know the power spiritual disciplines and mindfulness practices have to reduce anxiety, depression, and worry. Wholeness and salvation, which both derive from the same Greek root word, *sozo*, meaning "whole" or "healed," are found by being fully present to the grace and love of God. Prayerful meditation practices have opened generations to the abundant life God also offers each of us. Soaked in grace, we continually learn to lean into and quiet our thoughts and emotions while we cherish the bodies we have been given. Through these practices we embrace that we are loved, and we seek to offer ourselves to others out of this love. We deeply believe our well-being and wholeness are linked to yours, and we hope these tools will bless your life.

Within these pages, faith, practice, and science come together. We not only share our own experiences but the science behind how intentional mindfulness practices reduce anxiety, worry, and depression to develop a sense of wellness..Working through this guide each week will add new insight to your understanding of wellness. Over the course of eight weeks, you will connect to your own mind and body, expand your understanding of the importance of connection to others, develop your connection to nature, and then combine all these practices to build a resilient, joyful, and awakened life.

This guide also walks you through various exercises, journal prompts, discussion questions, and group activities. All audio tracks, video clips, and relevant website links mentioned in this guide can be accessed on the accompanying website, www.theawakenedlife.info. Each week leads you to explore ways in which you can better connect with God and see what God is doing in you, your relationships, and creation. Here is what you can expect each week:

Week 1. Introduction to the Awakened Life

Week 2. Connecting to Self: Noticing Thoughts

Week 3. Connecting to Self: Being Present in the Body

Week 4. Connecting to Others: Working through Loneliness

Week 5. Connecting to Others: Working through Shame

Week 6. Connecting to Creation: Experiencing Awe of Nature

Week 7. Connecting to Creation: Sharing a Meal of Intention

Week 8. Closing: Awakening to Joy

Each week will follow the same rhythm by revisiting the following five themes:

AWAKE

This is an introductory section on waking up to the abundant life God offers each of us. Each week you will practice a mindfulness awakening exercise. Sitting in silence with your thoughts and feelings can be weird, awkward, unfamiliar, and uncomfortable at first. You'll probably be frustrated or feel as though you're not doing it right. Please show yourself grace and remind yourself this is a process of training your mind to be awake to the present. Connect to your breath, remembering God breathed life into your lungs, as each breath offers the possibility for intimate connection with the Holy Spirit. Try not to judge your thoughts; instead, simply notice thoughts as they arise. Be curious about your amazing mind. This is a lifelong process and worth the effort.

AWARE

Each week, this section creates an awareness of what holds you back from abundant life, revealing scientific studies and real-life examples that illustrate the devastating reality of what living an anxious, disconnected life does to the body and mind. Naming your distractions, conflicts, and anxieties will begin to remove their power over your life.

ALIVE

This section provides group activities and discussions. The group will process together how to use the practices to be whole people. Through the various activities offered, the group will breathe, think, speak, and move intimately connected to God, others, and nature.

ΛBIDE

Weekly, this section offers a Christian spiritual practice handed down through the generations. Each practice is a means of experiencing divine, unconditional love. These grace-filled practices help us abide deeply in God's love for us, and they help restore the image of God in us all. If you do not identify as Christian, we invite you to adjust the practice to speak to your own faith tradition and we offer various ways to adapt this practice throughout.

ΛRISE

This weekly section offers a summary of the session and the week's practices to be completed between sessions. We know you have homework for your classes and are busy with all kinds of activities and work, but keep in mind that these mindfulness practices and spiritual disciplines bring calm and clarity when you use them. They are tools that will help you be present to your other obligations. Here are some tips to help you practice:

- Find a partner who is also in this group. You can check on each other during the week and encourage each other to practice your spiritual disciplines and mindfulness exercises.
- Set an alarm on your phone for the same time every day, to remember to practice. You can always listen to the online audio tracks at home as you practice.
- Make sure to complete the practice reflection journals as part of your daily routine.
- Extend grace to yourself, because everyone feels awkward when they start these practices. Your life will be better for your effort. The more you invest in this process, the more you will benefit, so please do the practices!

OUR HOPES

At the end of the eight weeks, we pray these practices and insights will help you cultivate joy and hope for your entire life. During the sessions, you will experience a variety of life-giving practices. Please reach for these practices throughout your day, when thoughts and emotions start to overwhelm you. Mindfulness and spiritual practices will bring calm and remind you of the beauty life offers. God is working in and through you right now, so we hope you stay awake and connected, and live each moment fully.

Your sisters,

and *Angie*

INTRODUCTION TO THE AWAKENED LIFE

AWAKE

Even after your alarm clock jars you awake in the morning and you get out of bed, do you ever feel as if you sleepwalk through your day? Do you go through the motions of your day not fully awake and present to the power of each moment? Does fear, worry, or self-consciousness keep you from experiencing joy in your day-to-day life? Do your thoughts wander? Does technology take your focus away from the people and events that are right in front of you? Pause for a moment to think about these questions. Take inventory of how awake you feel to your life.

Pause

Our time together will be spent seeking abundant life. The term *abundant life* describes a state of well-being, health, connection, wholeness, salvation, and ultimately, wakefulness. Unfortunately, many of us miss out on living an abundant life because we focus on negative things that happened in the past, or we worry about things that might happen in the future. This tendency causes us to miss the fullness and joy that are at our fingertips. Abundant life does not mean life without struggle or pain, but rather a life deeply connected to what God is doing in the moment—in you, in your relationships with others, and in creation. When living an abundant life, resiliency and joy are accessible, even in the midst of struggle. Let's take a couple of minutes to watch a video of Dr. Amy Oden describing abundant life. This video can be found at www.the awakenedlife.info.

Video: Abundant Life—Dr. Amy Oden

Group Activity

Part of awakening to the world around us involves getting to know each other. To foster this, break off into pairs. Ask each other the following questions, and listen carefully for your partner's answers.

- What is your name?
- How do you wake up in the morning (alarm, snooze, no snooze, other)?
- Describe a moment in your life when you felt fully present and awake to something wonderful that was happening.

Awake Exercise

Awakening to God working in and through you in the present moment takes practice. Each week we will take time to pause and be present, listen to our breathing, and notice what is going on in our minds and bodies without judgment. If meditative prayer and mindfulness are not already part of your daily life, it may be difficult for you, initially, to sit in silence, and that's OK. Be kind to yourself as you learn and grow in this practice.

Audio Track 1: Opening Meditation—Dr. Sarah Bollinger, LCSW

Follow along and listen to the audio track online at www.theawakenedlife .info. Your group leader can also read this aloud.

Take a moment and find a comfortable, upright position. Sit with a straight spine, and gently rest both feet on the ground, legs uncrossed. Or, if you prefer, sit cross-legged on the floor. Rest your hands comfortably on your knees or in your lap. If you feel comfortable doing so, begin by closing your eyes. If not, simply rest your gaze on one unmoving spot a few feet in front of you.

Begin to notice your breath. Notice the ins and outs of each breathing cycle. Without judgment, just notice the quality of your breath. Is it shallow? Or heavy? Is it raspy? Or short? Without trying to change anything about your breath, take a couple of moments to notice it.

As you sit breathing, you may notice that your mind begins to wander. That's OK. Without judging yourself, simply take account of when you begin to get lost in thought and gently bring your mind back to the breath.

Take a minute to practice being with your breath.

Together as a group, let's all take one deep inhalation and an openmouthed exhalation; then slowly open your eyes when you are ready.

Awake Prayer

Let's say this prayer together as we end the exercise:

God, help me be fully present and thankful for each breath. This we pray, amen.

Group Check-In

How did it feel to do this meditation?

The Why

Did you know one in five college students live with a mental illness? It is not uncommon for students today to cope with depression, anxiety, and other mental health issues. In addition, the transition and stress associated with going to college bring great challenges. There is pressure to find life's purpose, get good grades, pay for school, take care of your apartment/dorm, and make friends. Students struggle with a darkness that drains color from their world in a host of ways. Anxiety and depression may be part of your life as well. If so, hear this clearly—you are not alone. This is nothing to be ashamed of, and there is hope.

Fortunately, there are strategies to achieve well-being that can help build resiliency and strength. Mindfulness, personal spiritual practices, healthy relationships, and time in nature have all been scientifically proven to improve mental and emotional health. During our time together, we will explore a number of mindfulness and spiritual practices that help us stay well. Mindfulness practices, like the breathing exercise we did together earlier, invite us to take one moment at a time and fully live in the present. We will build an awakened life together through this and other simple, life-giving practices.

Note: Please remember: our time together over the next eight weeks does not replace medicine and counseling, which are important and effective treatments for anxiety and depression.

Group Reflection

- What are your initial reactions to mindfulness and spiritual practices?
- What experiences have you had in the past with mindfulness and spiritual practices?

"If one member suffers, all suffer together with it; if one member is honored, all rejoice together with it. Now you are the body of Christ and individually members of it."

1 CORINTHIANS 12:26-27, NRSV

Covenant

Connecting to self, others, and creation takes time and effort. It requires being real about your experiences, hopes, and dreams. This means being vulnerable and authentic. Creating a safe place for sharing and growing together also requires covenant. In the Judeo-Christian tradition, covenant means making a promise to each other and to God. Such a covenant is made up of vows you commit to as a group, which are a way to pledge respect and value one another. Together, we will create a covenant that will guide our work of discovering the awakened life. After we complete our covenant, each of us will sign our name and live out the promises we make about how this group will be together.

- Together, complete the ROPES exercise described in the Leader Guide on page **117.**

STUDENT GUIDE WEEK 1

- Ask one another, "What needs to be included in our covenant to create a safe place for you to share, heal, and grow into the person God created you to be?"

> "Whatever affects one directly, affects all indirectly. I can never be what I ought to be until you are what you ought to be, and you can never be what you ought to be until I am what I ought to be."
>
> **MARTIN LUTHER KING JR., "LETTER FROM A BIRMINGHAM JAIL"**

Journal Prompt

Free writing is an exercise that prompts you to write whatever comes to mind, without judgment or editing. Take five minutes and journal about the questions that follow. Don't worry about spelling or grammar. Just allow yourself time to brainstorm without filtering your thoughts.

1. When have you felt most whole/well in your life? This may have been at a specific event or during a time period when you felt a general sense of well-being.
2. What is well-being? Wholeness? Salvation?
3. When have you felt closest to God, and how did it impact you?
4. What keeps you from feeling whole/well in your life?

_____

_____

_____

_____

_____

_____

_____

_____

_____

_____

_____

_____

_____

_____

Group Discussion

After five to ten minutes of journaling, share your responses as a large group. You can share as much or as little as you want. Use what you wrote down as a guide.

ABIDE

This week's spiritual practice is an ancient Christian practice called _lectio divina_. _Lectio divina_ means "divine reading" and includes focused reading, meditation, and prayer. This practice starts with a prayer inviting the Holy Spirit to reveal something to you through the experience.

Find a quiet place in the room or outside to spend time with God. During this session, choose a scripture from the following list. You are also free to choose your own scripture. Or, if you do not identify as Christian, you can utilize this process with other writings from your faith tradition or use one of the poems suggested below as a focus text. We also recommend using this same scripture or poem each day this week during your home practices to deepen your understanding and experience of the text.

1. Jesus said, "I came that they may have life, and have it abundantly." (John 10:10, NRSV)

2. Genesis 1:27

3. Psalm 139:13-14

4. Matthew 11:28-30

5. Excerpt from Hafiz, "Awake Awhile":

    > Awake, my dear.
    > Be kind to your sleeping heart.
    > Take it out into the vast fields of Light
    > And let it breathe.

6. Excerpt from John O'Donohue, "The Question Holds the Lantern":

    "Once you start to awaken, no one can ever claim you again for the old patterns. . . . You want your God to be wild and to call you to where your destiny awaits."

To practice lectio divina, read through the selected scripture or poem excerpt three times. The first time, read it slowly in your mind. The second time, read it slowly out loud. The third time, read it again in your mind, noting which words impress themselves upon you the most. Then spend quiet time listening for God's still, small voice, noting further what the passage says to you. Write in your journal if it helps you process what you hear. At the end of this practice, pay attention to how the insights you gained can impact your health and well-being.

Today we learned about the importance of being awake, aware, and alive in the moment. Next week, we will dig into the incredibly and uniquely beautiful person God has created you to be. Before we meet again, it's important to practice regularly what you have learned thus far. In order to notice lasting change, regular practice is key. Make sure to check out the tips for establishing a regular practice in the preface to maximize your efforts.

Home Practices for the Week

1. Practice the Awake exercise every day for 3 minutes.

2. Try the Abide spiritual practice (lectio divina) every day for 3 minutes.

3. Check in with your partner at least twice this week.

4. Keep track of your efforts in the journal area that follows. For example, "Day 1, [date], I practiced the Awake exercise and lectio divina." Then record your thoughts, emotions, and any physical sensations you notice. Keep in mind that there is no wrong answer. Just try it.

_____

_____

_____

_____

_____

_____

_____

_____

_____

_____

_____

_____

_____

_____

_____

_____

_____

_____

Closing Blessing

At the end of each session, we will share this unison blessing.

We are awakening to abundant life.
We are becoming aware of our worth and belonging.
We are coming alive to our senses, thoughts, and emotions.
We are abiding in the love and grace of God.
We arise now to live a life as connected, whole people.

CONNECTING TO
SELF

NOTICING THOUGHTS

This week we will discuss the beauty of our minds and the necessity of training ourselves to monitor our thought life in order to tune in to that deeper voice within. It might be helpful to review the ROPES exercise from last week as we begin and check in with each other about the ways we agree to create space for open and honest sharing in the group. It's also important to talk about the things you've practiced between sessions as a reminder. With this in mind, let's touch base:

- To get started, share a moment during the week when you felt most awake to your life.
- How did your home practices go?
- Reflecting on the journal entries you made between sessions, what do you notice about your body right now?

AWAKE

How cool is the mind—it keeps us alive! Our minds do everything from signaling our breathing to processing words when reading. Evolutionarily, we are designed to have our minds wander, to scan the horizon for danger, and to learn new things. It's OK for our minds to be busy, but sometimes our busy minds can get the best of us. Instead of making us more aware of our surroundings, our anxious and negative thoughts take us completely out of the moment. The truth is, we are more than our thoughts. Thoughts can be helpful, but ultimately our thoughts change from day to day, or even from moment to moment. When we think about past regrets or worry about the future, we miss the only moment we can truly be alive, which is now.

This week we will begin cultivating a healthy awareness of our thoughts. Think about all the things vying for our attention—worries, other people's expectations, our consumer culture, advertising, even cell phones. All these demands for our attention can be exhausting. Yet, we can train our minds in the same way that we train the muscles in our bodies. With training, we can notice our thoughts without allowing them to rob us of our present-moment awareness. It is through cultivating this attention that we find amazing freedom to focus on what is truly important to us.

"Thoughts and beliefs are navigational maps that are not inherently true. Rather, some serve us and others cause feelings of separation, self-aversion, and/or blame of others. We can free ourselves from harmful beliefs by investigating them with a dedicated, mindful and courageous presence."

TARA BRACH

14

Awake Conversation

Take a moment to search for and read the poem "The Summer Day" by Mary Oliver, which is available here: www.loc.gov/poetry/180/133.html. This is a lovely example of paying attention and experiencing the blessing of life in the present moment. Two lines in this poem speak powerfully of cultivating our awareness and paying attention to the simple things that are right in front of us. Oliver writes that she doesn't know what a prayer is, but she does know "how to pay attention, how to fall down / into the grass . . ."

- What do these lines mean to you?
- Where or when do you know how to pay attention?

Awake Exercise

Just as we did last week, we are going to take some time to practice and train our minds to focus on the still, small voice of God. This is not a onetime experience but a journey. This is an opportunity to notice our thoughts without judgment and hear our inner voices above the noise of the world.

Audio Track 2: Awareness Meditation—Dr. Sarah Bollinger, LCSW

Follow along and listen to the audio track online at www.theawakenedlife .info. Your group leader can also read this aloud.

Once again, begin by finding a relaxed but upright position. Sit with a straight spine with your back resting against a chair, or sit cross-legged on the floor. Rest your hands comfortably on your knees or in your lap. Close your eyes and begin to focus on your breath.

Begin to notice your breath. Notice the ins and outs of each breathing cycle. Without judgment, just notice the quality of your breath. Is it shallow? Or heavy? Is it raspy? Or short? Without trying to change anything about your breath, take a couple of moments and just be with it.

As you bring awareness to your breath, allow your mind to gently relax. When you notice that your mind begins to wander and thoughts take you away from the present moment, without judgment, gently bring your mind back to the breath. As you notice thoughts come and go, you can think of your thoughts as clouds in a big, blue, open sky. As thoughts come, notice that, just as clouds float through the sky, your thoughts float through your mind, leaving a clear, blue sky behind. Try not to attach too much attention to each thought cloud; allow thoughts to come and gently go, coming back to an awareness of your breath whenever you need to. Take a moment to practice.

As you are ready, slowly open your eyes and bring your attention back to the room.

Awake Prayer

Let's say this prayer together as we end the exercise:

God, help me notice my own thoughts and be thankful for my mind. This we pray, amen.

Group Check-In

Pair up with a partner and share your answers to the following questions.

- What were thoughts that you noticed during the meditation?
- What were your reactions to your thoughts?

AWARE

Why

Why is being aware of our thoughts important to our mental and spiritual health and well-being? One Harvard study reveals, "People spend 46.9 percent of their waking hours thinking about something other than what they're doing, and this mind-wandering typically makes them unhappy."[1] This means almost half of the time our thoughts take us out of the moment. This disconnection feeds our sense of being unwell.

Thoughts can be distracting and overwhelming, but ultimately, thoughts are just thoughts. They are real but not always true. In other words, thoughts are not always facts. They come and go, and they often change like the wind. We can monitor the content of our thoughts to keep ourselves well. Noticing and naming mental activities and thought patterns, specifically those negative activities and thought patterns that grab hold of our minds, is key to minimizing their power over our lives.

Negative Thought Patterns

Here are some examples of negative thought patterns that you may experience in your life:

- Catastrophizing—jumping to the worst-case scenario
- Mind reading—assuming what others are thinking, without knowing their real thoughts
- The "shoulds"—feeling as if you need to do something because of some unwritten rule
- Personalizing—making everything about yourself, even if it is unrelated to you
- Blaming—holding others responsible for your own pain and suffering

- Being the eternal expert—not allowing yourself to be wrong or to make mistakes[2]

Aware Journaling

Now that you are aware of some of these negative thought patterns, take a few moments to look at them and write down any you have experienced in your own life. Do you recognize any of these negative thought patterns in yourself? What triggers these types of thoughts in you? Do you recognize these thought patterns in others? Family? Friends?

> "I've lived through some terrible things in my life, some of which actually happened."
>
> **MARK TWAIN**

Group Conversation

As you feel comfortable, share your reflections from the journal exercise.

- What did you notice about your thought patterns?
- Was there a time when you practiced catastrophizing or mind reading but later discovered there was no threat, or that you "misread" another's mind?

Group Exercise

Read the following example and discuss as a group what negative thought patterns are at work in this scenario.

Lauren was walking across campus yesterday and saw her friend Rachel across the quad. They hadn't seen each other in several days, and Lauren was excited to connect. Lauren looked up and waved, but Rachel kept her head down, walking quickly on to class. Immediately, Lauren started thinking about the worst-case scenarios: "Is Rachel mad at me? Why didn't she come over to talk to me or at least wave back? What did I say when I was with her last? Maybe I said something that offended her, or maybe she's just being a jerk." Lauren walked on to class and couldn't stop thinking about how Rachel had acted all day. This interaction impacted her mood for the rest of the afternoon, making her crabby and anxious.

- Lauren struggles with which negative thought patterns?
- What could Lauren do instead to bring awareness to these negative thought patterns?

> "Teacher, which is the greatest commandment in the Law?" Jesus replied: "'Love the Lord your God with all your heart and with all your soul and with all your mind.' This is the first and greatest commandment. And the second is like it: 'Love your neighbor as yourself.'"
>
> **MATTHEW 22:36-39, NIV**

Teaching Moment: Self-Compassion

God's greatest commandment in the New Testament instructs us to love God with our whole being and our neighbor as ourselves. Yet all too often, loving ourselves and showing ourselves compassion is not something we practice. When we take time to notice our own thoughts, we often judge them or try to change them. This is where practicing mindful self-compassion is crucial to well-being.

According to psychologist Kristin Neff, self-compassion has three elements:

1. Self-kindness rather than self-judgment
2. Mindfulness rather than over-identification with our thoughts
3. Recognizing our common humanity rather than isolating ourselves[3]

Group Discussion

Ponder these questions and share them with the group:

- Have you been able to practice self-kindness rather than self-judgment?
- How can you greet negative thoughts with compassion and curiosity rather than judgment and fear?
- Since thoughts can be negative and fleeting, how can you be mindful of them but not overidentify with them?
- How might recognizing our common humanity help us to be compassionate with ourselves?

Group Exercise

Take a few moments to read "The Guest House" by Jellaludin Rumi, below:

> This being human is a guest house.
> Every morning a new arrival.
>
> A joy, a depression, a meanness,
> some momentary awareness comes
> as an unexpected visitor.
>
> Welcome and entertain them all!
> Even if they are a crowd of sorrows,
> who violently sweep your house
> empty of its furniture,
> still, treat each guest honorably.
> He may be clearing you out
> for some new delight.
>
> The dark thought, the shame, the malice.
> meet them at the door laughing and invite them in.
>
> Be grateful for whatever comes.
> because each has been sent
> as a guide from beyond.
>
> —Jellaludin Rumi, translation by Coleman Barks

Group Conversation

Take a few minutes to share your insights from "The Guest House." Use the following questions to guide your conversation.

- Is welcoming your thoughts and emotions uncomfortable for you, or freeing?
- If they are unwelcome, why?
- If they are freeing, describe this freedom.

> "Talk to yourself the way you'd talk to someone you love."
>
> BRENÉ BROWN

 ABIDE

This week's spiritual practice is "the practice of the presence of God." This practice was inspired by Brother Lawrence, a monk who was able to train his mind to find joy and peace in daily, routine life, no matter how rote or how much he initially disliked a task. He found every moment of life, every activity, was an opportunity to be in the presence of God. As noted by Dr. Amy Oden, "This shifted his frame of reference for all daily work, no longer seeking others' approval or striving toward a goal, and instead the purpose was being with and loving God."[4] John Wesley, founder of the Methodist movement, said the character of a Methodist is this: "He is therefore happy in God, yea, always happy, as having in him 'a well of water springing up into everlasting life,' and overflowing his soul with peace and joy. 'Perfect love' having now 'cast out fear,' he 'rejoices evermore.'"[5] Intentionally practicing the presence of God creates a life of gratitude and joy for each precious moment of life.

Abide Practice

Here are some simple steps for the practicing of the presence of God:

1. Take a moment to think and share with one another about the tasks you do in your daily life.

2. Break out with your partner and pick one task to focus on this week. Examples might be brushing your teeth or washing the dishes. Read through the rest of the instructions and talk with your partner about how you might bring more intention to this task.

3. Each time you do this task, use your Awake practices from this guide to open yourself to God's presence in the moment. Breathe, and notice your feelings and emotions—how you experience them in your body. Then continually bring your focus back, asking, How is God with me in these moments? How can I experience and share God's love through this task? How can God open me to joy and peace through this task? Answer these questions with your partner, and stay in prayerful conversation with God while accomplishing this task during the week. Check in with each other throughout the week.

4. Give God thanks for your ability to complete this task, and soak in the love God gives you with each breath.

5. Expand this practice until it is part of your entire life. This will increase your connection to God, yourself, others, and nature, so you may experience joy, peace, and hope continually.[6]

"The most simple spiritual discipline is some degree of solitude and silence. But it's the hardest, because none of us want to be with someone we don't love. . . . We won't have the courage to go into that terrifying place of the soul without a great love, without the light and love of the Lord. Such silence is the most spacious and empowering technique in the world, yet it's not a technique at all. It's precisely the refusal of all technique."

RICHARD ROHR

ARISE

Today we learned about awakening to our minds and the importance of self-compassion. If we do not regularly train our minds, they easily become weak and distracted, just like our other muscles. Use the home practices, and begin to get curious about how your mind works.

Home Practices for This Week

1. Practice your Awake exercise each day for 3 minutes.

2. Follow the Awake exercise with one minute of self-compassion.

3. Try the Abide practice every day while accomplishing a simple task, such as brushing your teeth in the morning and at night.

4. Check in with your partner at least twice this week.

5. Keep track of your efforts in the journal area that follows. For example, "Day 1 [date], I practiced the Awake and Abide practices." Then record your thoughts, emotions, and any physical sensations you notice. Keep in mind that there is no wrong answer.

_____

_____

_____

_____

_____

_____

_____

_____

_____

_____

_____

_____

_____

_____

_____

_____

Closing Blessing

At the end of each session, we will share this unison blessing.

We are awakening to abundant life.
We are becoming aware of our worth and belonging.
We are becoming alive to our senses, thoughts, and emotions.
We are abiding in the love and grace of God.
We arise now to live a life as connected, whole people.

CONNECTING TO
SELF

BEING PRESENT IN THE BODY

This week we awaken to the beauty and power of our bodies. Before we start, let's check in regarding our group dynamics and about your weekly practices. It is important to practice what you learn each week.

- How are we doing on making this a place to openly share and be fully present?
- What did you notice while working through the home practices?
- As you reflect on your home practices log, what do you notice about your body's reaction right now?

AWAKE

Have you ever taken time to marvel at the miracle of your own body? Your eyes perceive the smile of a friend, the glorious colors of a masterpiece, funny cat videos, and the majesty of the mountains. Your nose breathes in the comforting smell of bread baking, the joy of a puppy's breath, the scent of freshly laundered clothes, and the fragrance of a budding flower. Your ears soak in the extraordinary insights of a great teacher, your own

27

voice speaking your truth, your joyful singing in your car, and the precious moment when you hear the words "I love you." Our mouths open to the sweetness of honey, the tartness of cherries, the nourishment of kale, the pleasure of macaroni and cheese, and the communion of a shared meal. Our skin intimately connects us to the delight of goose bumps–inducing music, the power of clicking on a text message, the shelter of a hug, and the soul-touching nature of a kiss.

Not only does your body make all these sensual experiences possible; it also allows you to connect with your mind and soul. This mind, body, soul connection is crucial to wholeness. Your body signals you when you are hungry, tired, anxious, hurt, and sad. If you do not pay attention to these signals, you become bogged down and unwell. If ignored, these bodily experiences can lead to spiraling thoughts, and it becomes easy to forget you are a precious child of God, designed with all the tools necessary to live abundantly. God's breath is in you, and you are fearfully and wonderfully made. You were created with the ability to know when you need to nourish, rest, heal, protect, and soothe your body. Just paying attention and trusting yourself enough to follow the cues your body sends is the key. This week, you will focus on paying attention to what your body reveals to you about healthy ways to live. Again, this takes practice, but it is worth the effort.

Awake Exercise

This week we will practice an exercise called the Raisin Meditation. Sarah will walk us through the full-body sensory experience of tasting a raisin. You will hold, see, touch, smell, feel, taste, swallow, and follow the raisin in your body. Remember: all these awake experiences may feel strange and awkward at first, but they enhance your experience of life and connection to your body and soul.

"[Jesus] said to them, 'Come away to a deserted place all by yourselves and rest a while.' For many were coming and going, and they had no leisure even to eat."

MARK 6:31, NRSV

Audio Track 3: Raisin Meditation—Dr. Sarah Bollinger, LCSW

You may choose to listen to the audio track, found at www.theawakened life.info, or have the leader read this aloud to the group.

1. **Holding**: First, take a raisin and hold it in the palm of your hand.

2. **Seeing**: Take time to really look at it; focus on the raisin with intention, and gaze at it with care and full attention. Imagine that you have never seen an object like this before in your life. Let your eyes explore every part of it, examining the highlights where the light shines, the darker hollows, the folds and ridges, and any asymmetries or unique features.

3. **Touching**: Turn the raisin over between your fingers and explore its texture. You might close your eyes if that enhances your sense of touch.

4. **Smelling**: Hold the raisin beneath your nose. With each inhalation, take in any smell, aroma, or fragrance that may arise. As you do this, notice anything interesting that may be happening in your mouth or stomach.

5. **Placing**: Now slowly bring the raisin up to your lips. Gently place the raisin in your mouth; without chewing, notice how it gets into your mouth in the first place. Spend a few moments focusing on the sensations of having it in your mouth.

6. **Tasting**: When you are ready, prepare to chew the raisin. Very consciously, take one or two bites into it and notice what happens in the aftermath, experiencing any waves of taste as you continue chewing. Without swallowing yet, notice the sensations of taste and texture in your mouth.

7. **Swallowing**: When you feel ready to swallow the raisin, see if you can first detect the intention to swallow as it comes to you, so that even this is experienced consciously before you swallow the raisin.

8. **Following**: Finally, see if you can feel what is left of the raisin moving down into your stomach, and sense how your body is feeling after you have completed this exercise.[7]

Prayer

Let's say this prayer together as we end the exercise:

God, help me notice my own thoughts and emotions, and then be thankful for how I experience them in my body. This we pray, amen.

Group Check-In

Pair up with a partner and share your answers to the following questions.

- Which of the steps in this experience seemed strange and which were enjoyable?
- How do you think being awake in this way is important to well-being and wholeness?

For some of us, being present, staying "in the now," is excruciating or seemingly impossible. Sometimes when we experience how our thoughts and feelings impact our bodies, our tendency is to numb out. In your life this tendency may result in binge-watching videos or sports, drinking too much, gossiping, or getting on social media to avoid the difficulties presented to us in life.

Smartphone technology is one of the things we reach for to avoid pain. Our smartphones have the potential to keep us connected to people and give us access to vast amounts of information and entertainment, but many people report these advantages as isolating. In a poignant *Psychology Today* article, a student shares his experience at dinner with some friends.

> Speaking of being tethered and isolating myself, just a few nights ago I went out to eat with my friends, and half the time we were at the restaurant I was constantly checking my phone; in fact I was too busy checking my own to even notice if anyone else had been looking at theirs. For some parts of the conversation I just gave short replies or nods to the conversation because I was missing what was actually being said. Even watching this video for class, I had to stop and rewind a few times because I found myself getting distracted by my phone.[8]

Aware Journaling

Take a few moments to journal the answers to the following three questions.

1. Does this story resonate with you?

2. If you are spending this much time on your phone, what is missing from your life?

3. What are you avoiding and not noticing about your thoughts and emotions? How does this impact your body?

_____

_____

_____

_____

_____

_____

_____

_____

_____

_____

_____

_____

_____

_____

_____

_____

This avoidance and numbing of our senses has dire consequences on our bodies. Avoidance can manifest as anxiety, and in turn we carry this stress knowingly and unknowingly in our bodies. The Mayo Clinic notes that stress can impact the body in the following ways: headaches, muscle tension, chest pains, fatigue, change in sex drive, stomachaches, sleep problems, change in mood, anxiety, restlessness, lack of motivation or focus, irritability or anger, sadness, depression, and feeling overwhelmed. These stresses also lead to negative behaviors, such as overeating and undereating, angry outbursts, drug or alcohol abuse, tobacco use, social withdrawal, and exercising less.[9]

The good news is, our bodies are our connection to the present, because the body gives us the best information about what is happening inside us right now. Instead of numbing and shutting out these messages, we can learn to sit with our own thoughts and feelings and experience how they impact our bodies. Nourishing our bodies and taking care of them are intimately connected to well-being in this way.

Group Discussion

Think about the relationship between bodily sensations, thoughts, emotions, and behaviors. For example, has your stomach ever growled, followed by you having the thought, *I should eat*, but you don't? Then your thoughts begin to spiral negatively, and you angrily snap at your friend, who has done nothing wrong? Take a few moments to answer the following questions in groups of two to three people as we discuss our mind-body connection together.

- Can you name a time when you did not listen to the signals your body was giving you?
- Describe what happened both in your body and in your response to the world around you.
- If you could go back and pay attention to your body cues, how do you think the experience would be different?

Group Activity

As you think about your responses to the questions from the group discussion, participate in the following activity, which asks you to physically respond to a similar question: If one wall of the room you are in represents the statement, "I am in touch with my body, and I listen to what it tells me," and the opposite wall represents the statement, "I never listen to my body," where do you think you are in this range of experiences? Go stand in the place representing your experience.

Group Discussion

As a large group discuss the following questions related to the "I am connected to my body" exercise. Then follow the prompts for further discussion on the body-mind connection.

- Are you surprised with the range of positions noted in the room?
- What do you want to ask one another about where you are standing? Tell each other more.
- When you were five years old, where on the range do you think you would have stood? Move now to that place. Or are you in the same place? Why or why not?

Clench your fists as tightly as you can and hold them closed for 15 seconds; now unclench them. Notice what you feel in your hands.

- Describe the feeling.
- Notice how your hands feel internally—what sensations are you experiencing? Tingling? Warmth? Tension? Other?

Repeat this exercise, but instead of clenching your fists, smile for 15 seconds and then relax your face.

- Describe the feeling.
- How is this feeling different from clenching your fists?

Self-Compassion Teaching

Just as we talked about last week, compassion for ourselves is essential to well-being. Look through the following scenarios and be aware of where your thoughts go when these things happen:

- You ate a whole bag of chips or a pint of ice cream by yourself.
- You stayed up all night playing on your phone.
- You partied too hard and missed an important class the next morning.
- You canceled a get-together with a friend and stayed home instead to binge-watch videos.
- You failed a quiz.

Alive Journaling

Take a few moments to pick one of the scenarios above and process your thoughts. How do you feel in your body in relation to your thoughts? What happened in your mind and body when this scenario occurred? Did your inner critic kick in with a vengeance and cause your heart to race or your jaw to clench? Did it take you down a spiral of self-loathing? Did you feel sick in the pit of your stomach? *Or*, did your awake, compassionate self grow curious about your emotions and dig deeper for a positive way to respond? Did you begin to lovingly acknowledge your own stress, anxiety, fear, or pain? Did you speak words of encouragement and hope into your mind, breathe deep, and allow the tension to lessen? Did you acknowledge your need to rest, eat, or talk, and name your need? Did you remind yourself no one is perfect, so you do not have to be either?

_____

_____

_____

_____

_____

_____

_____

_____

_____

_____

_____

_____

_____

_____

_____

_____

Self-Compassion Exercise

We all face our own inner critics, but compassion can de-escalate the stress and isolation of the moment. This exercise may feel forced and awkward at first, but loving and knowing yourself are stepping-stones to abundant life. Ideally, stand in front of a mirror or take a selfie with your hand gently cradling your face, hug yourself, or place a comforting hand on your heart. Then say five loving things to yourself. This is an exercise you can do anytime and anyplace you feel anxious, as you can say the words in your head instead of aloud.

- How did this exercise feel?
- Was it challenging to find five loving things to say to yourself? Why or why not?

"There comes a time when it is vitally important for your spiritual health to drop your clothes, look in the mirror, and say, 'Here I am. This is the body-like-no-other that my life has shaped. I live here. This is my soul's address.'"

BARBARA BROWN TAYLOR

ABIDE

Audio Track 4: Christian Mindfulness Practice—Dr. Amy Oden

Dr. Amy Oden will walk you through the four steps of Christian mindfulness in this track. You may choose to listen to the audio track, found at www.theawakenedlife.info, or have your group leader read this aloud.

We begin Christian mindfulness practice with attentive breathing. So, take several slow, deep breaths, and notice as you breathe the feel of your chest as it rises and falls, the sensation of air in your nose and lungs. Fully experience breathing, this gift God gives you in every breath.

As you continue to breath mindfully, bring your attention to your embodiment. Let your breathing fill your whole body as you visualize oxygen filling your lungs, your torso, your arms and legs. Focus your attention on the sensations or feelings or attitudes that you may find as you scan your body . . . perhaps a tightness here, or a tingle there. But notice, from your head through your shoulders and arms, down through your torso, notice what arises. Sensations, feelings—be curious. You don't need to label or analyze it; just notice what's there, on through your lower torso, through your legs, down to your toes. Take a moment for attentive embodiment.

The third step of acknowledgment is to hold what arises, as you have noticed in your body. As each item, each sensation or feeling or attitude, arises in your body, take a moment to acknowledge it, to receive it nonjudgmentally and hold it before God. This is prayerful paying attention: to invite God to hold with us as we acknowledge whatever arises from our breathing and our embodiment.

And finally, discover what shifts or changes as you invite God to hold with you what you have noticed. Do thoughts or feelings shift? Does a sensation increase or diminish as you hold it with God? The point here is to discover how God's presence in our mindful breathing and mindful embodiment can help us discover. Breathe one more time, in and out, as we give thanks mindfully for God's presence with us.

ARISE

Today, we learned about awakening to our bodies and the importance of self-compassion. Use the home practices to begin to get curious about the connection between your body and your thoughts and emotions.

Home Practice for This Week

1. Practice your Awake exercise (raisin or other food mindfulness practice) each day for 3 minutes.

2. Follow the Awake exercise with one minute of self-compassion.

3. Try the Abide spiritual tradition (Christian mindfulness) every day for 3 minutes.

4. Check in with your partner at least twice this week.

5. Keep track of your efforts in the journal area that follows. For example, "Day 1 [date], I practiced the Awake and Abide practices." Then record your thoughts, emotions, and any physical sensations you notice. Keep in mind that there is no wrong answer.

Closing Blessing

At the end of each session, we will share this unison blessing.

We are awakening to abundant life.
We are becoming aware of our worth and belonging.
We are becoming alive to our senses, thoughts, and emotions.
We are abiding in the love and grace of God.
We arise now to live a life as connected, whole people.

CONNECTING TO OTHERS

WORKING THROUGH LONELINESS

This week we are expanding our awareness to the power of connecting to others. Before we dig in, it is time to check in regarding our covenant to make this a welcoming place to share and grow, and your home practices. It is so important to practice what we learn each week. So, how is it going?

- How are we doing on creating a place to be fully present and willing to share your thoughts?
- What did you notice about your thoughts and emotions while doing your practices between sessions?
- As you read and reflect on your practice journal entries, what do you notice about your body right now?

AWAKE

Over the last three weeks, you began the work of awakening to God's presence in and through your mind and body. By noticing and listening to your own thoughts and feelings, you are beginning to experience compassion and grace for yourself and embracing your infinite value. You are quieting negative thoughts and diminishing the distractions, which is making space to experience your extraordinary connection to God's abundant life as defined in Week 1. Hopefully you are recognizing or remembering that you are a beloved child of God who is covered by God's grace. This grace is the unconditional love and transforming power of God given freely to you and available to tap into each moment.

Our next step is making space to hear and experience God by connecting to other people. As you quiet your mind and remove distractions, you can begin to make space for others. As you recognize you are a beloved child of God, you also realize this love extends to everyone else. As you sense God working in and through you, you can celebrate how God is also working in and through them. As you embrace your own inherent worth, you can acknowledge the inherent worth of others and build healthy, whole relationships.

Awake Exercise

We are created to be in relationship with one another. Just like being awake and present to yourself, truly being present with others is a skill we cultivate over years. Let's practice again pausing and connecting to ourselves, so we can open ourselves to others.

This exercise begins by cultivating loving-kindness for ourselves and then moves to extend that loving-kindness to others around us. Clinical psychologist and meditation instructor Tara Brach states, "The loving-kindness (*metta*, in Pali) meditation awakens us to our connectedness with all of life. Often the starting place is an offering of care to our own being. . . . By regarding ourselves with kindness, we begin to dissolve the identity of an isolated, deficient self. This creates grounds for including others in an unconditionally loving heart."[10]

Audio Track 5: Loving-Kindness Meditation 1—Dr. Sarah Bollinger, LCSW

Follow along and listen to the audio track, found at www.theawakenedlife .info. Your group leader can also read this aloud.

Sit comfortably in an upright position and take a few moments to get in touch with your breath and your body. As we have done in previous weeks, begin by focusing on your breath. Notice your breath in this moment. Imagine breathing in loving warmth and energy, and breathing out anything that is keeping you from being present. Take a moment to be with your breath. Then notice any areas of your body that might be holding tensions and gently relax these areas. As we begin, start by tuning in to a sense of softness and compassion for yourself. And then simply repeat these few phrases to yourself.

> May I feel safe.
> May I be physically happy.
> May I know the natural joy of being alive.
> May I be filled with loving-kindness.
> May I be free.

As you repeat each phrase in your mind, note any images, feelings, or sensations that come up. This might be difficult for you, but as you would treat your best friend, continue to imagine having this love for yourself. After you repeat these phrases a few times in your own mind, think of someone whom you love very much. Think of the qualities that you admire about them. Reflect on the things that you most appreciate about who they are. Begin to extend these phrases to them.

May they feel safe.
May they be physically happy.
May they know the natural joy of being alive.
May they be filled with loving-kindness.
May they be free.

Prayer

Let's say this prayer together as we end the exercise:

God, help me be fully present and thankful for the opportunity to share life with the people in this room. This we pray, amen.

Group Check-In

- How did it feel to participate in this practice?
- After a few weeks of completing this practice, what is it like now when you sit with your own thoughts, emotions, and bodily sensations?
- What do you need to let go of so you can be fully present?

AWARE

If we are unable to be with ourselves, be with our own angst, boredom, and emotions, how will this translate to friendships, family relationships, and love relationships? We will likely project our anxiety, fear, insecurities, and boredom onto the other person. We will make assumptions about what other people are thinking and feeling, but they are likely untrue and manifestations of our own baggage. When our low self-esteem and worries bump up against other people's struggles, relationships can seem too hard, and we may even give up on relationships. This is likely one of the reasons loneliness is experienced by so many people.

Cigna, the global insurance company, polled twenty thousand US adults using the UCLA Loneliness Scale.

"Loneliness is defined as a feeling of being alone or lacking social con-nectedness," Douglas Nemecek, M.D., chief medical officer for Behav-ioral Health at Cigna, told CBS News. "At Cigna, we've been hearing more and more from our customers and individuals calling us that they're feeling lonely, alone and disconnected from others."

. . . Generation Z, or those between the ages of 18 and 22, were the loneliest generation, with a "loneliness score" of 48.3. Possible loneli-ness scores range from 20 to 80, with the national average a 44.[11]

If you experience loneliness and disconnection, you are not the only one feeling it, and you can do something about it. Relationships are beautiful and messy. They take effort and intentionality but are worth the invest-ment and lead to experiences of true love, respect, and connection. Did you know science has proven that when individuals sing a song in a choir, the hearts of the singers begin to beat as one in rhythm with the music and with each other?[12] Interconnection is possible, and real.

"Solitude is very different from a 'time-out' from our busy lives. Solitude is the very ground from which community grows. Whenever we pray alone, study, read, write, or simply spend quiet time away from the places where we interact with each other directly, we are potentially opened for a deeper intimacy with each other."

HENRI NOUWEN

Group Discussion

Let's take some time to discuss when we have felt connected and disconnected. As a large group, consider the following questions:

- When have you felt most connected to others?
- When have you felt disconnected?
- What does it feel like to be connected?
- What does it feel like to be disconnected?
- When has disconnection happened through conflict?

Teaching Moment: Deep Listening

Growing closer in any relationship happens when we truly make space to hear the other person. This means listening to everything, from the mundane details of life to the depths of one's hopes and dreams. It is also an incredibly powerful way of leaning into conflict. Conflict is not necessarily a bad thing. Conflict can lead to growth, but this growth happens most profoundly when we truly hear each other.

Deep Listening Exercise

Let's take some time to practice deep listening. Move to a place where you can sit face-to-face in small groups of three. Each person will choose one of the categories below and share his or her own experience for 5 minutes without interruption. Switch roles and repeat the exercise, giving each person the chance to share and be heard for 5 minutes. When one person is speaking, try not to get distracted or even ask too many questions of the speaker; simply listen with as much intention as possible.

Describe a time when you experienced disconnection and/or conflict with:

- a family member
- a roommate
- an intimate relationship
- a friend
- a faculty member

Listeners, here are some key things to know and remember:

- Your role is to be quiet and present.
- Keep what you hear in confidence; trust is crucial.
- You are not to fix anything or offer advice.
- Cultivate curiosity. Be open to what you hear.
- If your mind wanders, gently reengage in listening. Remember: people deserve to be heard.

Sharer, here are some key things to know and remember:

- You are *invited* to share, not forced.
- This is a safe place, and what you say will be held in confidence.
- Speak from your own experience while respecting the experiences of others.
- Sharing your story is a powerful opportunity for healing and well-being.

Group Discussion

Come back to the larger group and share some of the highlights of your experience.

- What was it like for you to be the listener?
- What was it like for you to be the speaker?
- Can you see this practice helping in your relationships?

"Love is patient; love is kind;
love is not envious or boastful or
arrogant or rude. It does not insist
on its own way; it is not irritable
or resentful; it does not rejoice in
wrongdoing, but rejoices in the
truth. It bears all things, believes all
things, hopes all things, endures
all things. Love never ends."

1 CORINTHIANS 13:4-8, NRSV

ABIDE

Audio Track 6: The Great Commandment Mindfulness Practice —Dr. Amy Oden

Listen to the audio track online, found at www.theawakenedlife.info, or have your leader read this aloud to the group.

We begin the Great Commandment mindfulness practice with mindful breathing for a few moments. Allow yourself to be present to your breath in your nose as you breathe in slowly and deeply and fully. Be present to that breath as it fills your lungs and your whole body, in and out, this gift from God that you cannot earn. Now bring your awareness into your body. Notice thoughts, feelings, sensations that arise. Be attentive as you scan slowly from head to shoulders, to arms, attentive to whatever arrives, noticing what limbs or locations in your body are experiencing—sensations, feelings—continue your body scan.

As you continue to scan and notice what arises, acknowledge whatever arises and hold it with God, letting God's presence become more and more real to you in this moment. You might visualize God's hands, holding with you, whatever arises, or God sitting next to you as you notice what arises, and hold it with God. Feel God's loving gaze upon you, as God's own child. Be present with God and be present in God's love. Let God's loving gaze dwell on you as you hear these words, "You must love the Lord your God with all your heart, with all your being, and with all your mind. You must love your neighbor as you love yourself."

Notice in this present moment how you are opening to this love that you have for God, for neighbor, and for self, today, right now. Is that love opening in you? Do you feel it somewhere particular in your body? What are you aware of? If you find you cannot experience love for others, for God, or for self, that's OK. You don't have to force yourself to do this. Simply surrender to God's love for you and let God's loving gaze dwell upon you.

As you notice your love for God, neighbor, and self, let yourself sink more deeply down into this love, like a warm bath . . . sinking deeper into this love for God, for neighbor, and for self. You might want to visualize this experience, this love, as roots sinking down into the earth, taking root for nourishment, love rooted in place, anchored in your life. As you visualize those roots of love holding in the soil, you might also see the buds that spring forth in your heart and in your life.

We close with gratitude for whatever you have discovered in the Great Commandment mindfulness practice. Breathe in and breathe out, giving thanks to God. Amen.

Today, we expanded beyond self to awakening to our connection with others. Use the practices to begin to strengthen and deepen your connection to others.

Home Practices for This Week

1. Practice your Awake meditation (the Loving-Kindness Meditation) each day for 3 minutes.

2. Try the Abide spiritual practice (the Great Commandment Mindfulness Practice) every day for 3 minutes.

3. Consciously practice deep listening in your conversations each day.

4. Check in with your partner at least twice this week.

5. Keep track of your efforts in the journal area that follows. For example, "Day 1 [date], I practiced the Awake and Abide practices." Then record your thoughts, emotions, and any physical sensations you notice. Keep in mind that there is no wrong answer.

_____

_____

_____

_____

_____

_____

_____

_____

_____

_____

_____

_____

_____

_____

_____

_____

_____

_____

_____

_____

_____

_____

_____

Closing Blessing

At the end of each session, we will share this unison blessing.

We are awakening to abundant life.
We are becoming aware of our worth and belonging.
We are becoming alive to our senses, thoughts, and emotions.
We are abiding in the love and grace of God.
We arise now to live a life as connected, whole people.

CONNECTING TO OTHERS

WORKING THROUGH SHAME

This week, we will talk about the power of really sharing our authentic selves with other people. Before we get to that, it is time to check in regarding our covenant and practices. This week, as always, it is crucial for this group to be intentional about creating a place for people to openly share their thoughts and feelings. It is also so important to practice what we learn each week.

- How are we doing honoring the covenant we created during Week 1 to care for each other?
- How did working on self-compassion and doing your mindfulness exercises go this week? Is it getting easier to practice?
- As you look over your home practice journals, what insights do you gain?

Dear friends, let's love each other, because love is from God, and everyone who loves is born from God and knows God.

1 JOHN 4:7, CEB

AWAKE

Imagine waking up in the morning embraced by divine love. This love is a spring of living water gushing in your soul. You awake to an unshakable sense of worthiness and belonging. You have the courage to know and be known by other people. Authenticity of self, being who God created you to be, is a gift to others. It makes you the best friend, because you have empathy and compassion to share. You love with your whole heart, and you are grateful and joyful in the knowledge that you are enough.

This vision can be your life. In the language of faith, communion with God and others is possible. Intimacy and connection are key to the abundant life we have been seeking throughout all our weeks together. As in these past weeks, this seeking of abundant life requires us to be able to sit with our own thoughts and feelings. Then, as we quiet our own minds and know ourselves more clearly, we make room and space to hear God and open our lives to others.

"The truth is: Belonging starts with self-acceptance. Your level of belonging, in fact, can never be greater than your level of self-acceptance, because believing that you're enough is what gives you the courage to be authentic, vulnerable and imperfect."

BRENÉ BROWN

54

Awake Exercise

In this exercise you revisit the Loving-Kindness Meditation and expand upon it a bit, now with three other people in mind. To begin, extend kindness by speaking silent words of well-being to someone you love while picturing that person in your mind. Then move out to sending loving-kindness in the same way to someone with whom you have a neutral relationship. Finally, attempt to send loving-kindness to someone with whom you have a troubled relationship. Notice what feelings and emotions you experience during this exercise, without placing pressure on yourself, or judgment. If extending loving-kindness to someone with whom you have a difficult relationship becomes uncomfortable, simply return to extending love to the first person before concluding the exercise.

Audio Track 7: Loving-Kindness Meditation 2—Dr. Sarah Bollinger, LCSW

Follow along and listen to the audio track, found at www.theawakenedlife .info. Your group leader can also read this aloud.

> Begin by settling in, noticing your breath and relaxing your body. Bring to mind someone you love very much. Think of the qualities that you admire about them. Reflect on the things that you most appreciate about who they are. Begin to extend these phrases to them. As you repeat each phrase in your mind, note any images, feelings, or sensations that come up.
>
>> May they feel safe.
>> May they be physically happy.
>> May they know the natural joy of being alive.
>> May they be filled with loving-kindness.
>> May they be free.

Now expand your awareness to include someone who is a neutral person in your life. This might be someone you do not know well or an acquaintance—someone for whom you do not have strong feelings, one way or another. Begin to extend loving-kindness to this neutral person.

> May they feel safe.
> May they be physically happy.
> May they know the natural joy of being alive.
> May they be filled with loving-kindness.
> May they be free.

Last, if you are able, think of someone who has hurt or offended you or someone with whom you have a troubled or difficult relationship. Bring this person's face to mind and recall the common humanity that you share. Repeat these phrases regarding this person, and notice what thoughts and feelings come up within you.

> May they feel safe.
> May they be physically happy.
> May they know the natural joy of being alive.
> May they be filled with loving-kindness.
> May they be free.

Prayer

Let's say this prayer together as we end the exercise:

God, help me be fully present and thankful for the opportunity to share life with the people in this room. In this we pray, amen.

- How did it feel to extend loving-kindness to someone you love deeply?

- How did it feel to extend loving-kindness to an acquaintance or someone you know neutrally?
- How did it feel to extend loving-kindness to someone with whom you have a troubled or difficult relationship?

AWARE

Intimacy and connection require vulnerability. Dr. Brené Brown, who is a social work researcher, gives us insights into what holds us back from vulnerability and leads to disconnection in the following video. This video is available at https://www.ted.com/talks/brene_brown_on_vulnerability?language=en.

Video: "The Power of Vulnerability"—Brené Brown, TEDx

> "Shame is the intensely painful feeling that we are unworthy of love and belonging."
>
> BRENÉ BROWN

Sadly, shame is a universal experience, and holding on to shame keeps us from being vulnerable to others, which halts the potential for connection. If we continually think people will not love the real us, we are stuck in a painful cycle of loneliness and isolation. It is important to note: the difference between guilt and shame is the difference between "I did something bad" and "I am bad."[13] Guilt helps us acknowledge that we have acted in a way that does not live up to our standards and values, and as a result, we have caused hurt. Guilt challenges us to ask for forgiveness and make a change, creating an opportunity for growth. Shame paralyzes and locks us in a spiral of unworthiness.

Aware Journaling

Following are some common human concepts and experiences that require vulnerability and can sometimes trigger shame. Take a few minutes and brainstorm on your own about some of the automatic associations you may have with each of these things. What did you learn as a child about them? Were you taught openness about these things? How did shame show up or not?

Body Image

_____

_____

_____

_____

_____

_____

_____

_____

Sex and Physical Intimacy

_____

_____

_____

_____

_____

_____

_____

_____

Showing Emotion

_____

_____

_____

_____

_____

_____

_____

Gender Roles in Your Family of Origin

_____

_____

_____

_____

_____

_____

_____

Teaching Moment: Shame Triggers

Part of working through shame involves noticing those things that trigger shame within us. Brené Brown talks a lot about this in her work on shame. She states:

> The first element of shame resilience is recognizing shame and understanding our triggers. . . .
>
> When we can't recognize shame and understand our triggers, shame blindsides us. It washes over us, and we want to slink away and hide.
>
> In contrast, if we recognize our shame triggers, we can make mindful, thoughtful decisions about how we're going to respond to shame—before we do something that might make things worse.
>
> Shame has physical symptoms. These might include your mouth getting dry, time seeming to slow down, your heart racing, twitching, looking down, and tunnel vision. These symptoms are different from one person to the next. So if you learn your physical symptoms, you can recognize shame and get back on your feet faster.[14]

Personal Reflection Time

Take a few moments to process your shame triggers. It may be helpful to think about a specific time in your life when you experienced shame. Perhaps you felt shame regarding some of the triggers that you wrote about earlier in the "Aware" section. This is a time to awaken to how shame exists in your body and mind, and name it. Answer the following questions on your own:

How does shame live and feel in your body?

_____

_____

_____

_____

If shame were an animal, what would it look like?

_____

_____

_____

_____

Use the space below to write all the ways you would fill in this blank. "I am not _____ enough."

_____

_____

_____

_____

How do you speak to yourself when you feel shame?

_____

_____

_____

_____   _____

Teaching Moment: Shame Antidote

Shame is vicious in the moment, but there is an antidote for shame. "Shame . . . needs three things to grow exponentially [in our lives]: secrecy, silence, and judgment."[15] This is why these next moments in group discussion are crucial to overcoming shame and allowing for intimacy with others. This discussion will require vulnerability; at this vulnerable time remember our covenant. This is a space free of judgment that fosters deep listening. Sharing our stories is incredibly powerful and healing.

Group Discussion

- Being vulnerable and naming our shame are acts of courage that defeat shame, so take a few moments to share something powerful that has been revealed to you about your own sense of shame.
- How does it feel to share and bring your shame into the light?
- Offer an example of support to another. You are not fixing someone or minimizing another person's pain. Simply be with the person in his or her experience and offer your listening ear and support. Some things that you might say to another in the group are: "You are heard. You are courageous. You are seen and you are loved."

Our Abide spiritual practice for the week is communion. In The United Methodist Church, we believe communion is an invitation for *everyone* to experience the love and grace of God. It is a table open to all who long to connect with God, grow in faithfulness, and live in peace with others. It is a place of intimate belonging, acceptance, and love. God receives you just as you are in this moment and calls you *enough*, and not *only* enough but blessed with God's love and the company of these friends. Come with open hearts to receive this concrete expression of a divine mystery. This is a place to be known and to know God. If you do not identify as Christian or feel uncomfortable leading communion, we invite you to use the blessing at the end of this section as you offer one another love and connection through the sharing of something simple, like grapes and bread.

Communion Instructions

For this spiritual practice, your leader will say the words printed in normal text in the Great Thanksgiving Liturgy below, and you are asked to join by saying the words printed in bold. After the liturgy, you will be invited to share this communion meal with one another. Each person will receive communion by a process called *intinction*, meaning you will be handed a piece of bread and then invited to dip it into the cup of juice before taking it in to nourish your soul. You will then be asked to offer the same nourishment to the person beside you. As you share communion with the person to your left, here are some examples of words you can offer along with the bread and juice:

- "[Insert Person's Name], I offer you the love and peace of God."
- "[Insert Person's Name], this is a gift of grace and connection from God."
- "[Insert Person's Name], this is the body of Christ and the cup of salvation."

THE GREAT THANKSGIVING LITURGY

The Lord be with you.
And also with you.

Lift up your hearts.
We lift them up to the Lord.

Let us give thanks to the Lord our God.
It is right to give our thanks and praise.

Blessed are you, our grace-filled Creator,
    whose strong and loving arms encompass the universe,
    for with your eternal Word and Holy Spirit you are forever
        one God.
Through your Word you created all things and called them
        good,
    and in you we live and move and have our being.
You created all humanity in your image and designed us for
        relationship.
Even when your people doubt and struggle, you remain faithful
        to your covenant of forever love.
In response to our need you came to live among us, suffer our
        same hurts,
    and show us what love does and says through the Word
        made flesh in Jesus Christ.

And so, with your people on earth and all the company of
        heaven
    we praise your name and join their unending hymn:

Holy, holy, holy Lord, God of power and might,
    heaven and earth are full of your glory. Hosanna in the
        highest.
Blessed is the One who comes in the name of the Lord.
    Hosanna in the highest.

Holy are you, and blessed is Jesus Christ, who called you Abba,
    Father.

As a mother tenderly gathers her children,
   you embraced a people as your own
   and filled them with a longing for peace, belonging, and
      wholeness.
In Jesus' suffering and death you poured your life out for us
   destroying the power of guilt, shame and death.
You raised from the dead this same Jesus,
   in a profound expression of the eternal hope you offer us
      your Holy Spirit,
   teaching us nothing can separate us from your love and
      guidance, and
   making us the people of your new covenant of restored
      connection.

On a night long ago, Jesus gathered his friends for a last meal
   together before his death.
Jesus took bread, gave thanks to you, broke the bread, gave it
   to the disciples, and said:
"Take, eat; this is my body which is given for you.
Do this in remembrance of me."

When the supper was over Jesus took the cup,
   gave thanks to you, gave it to the disciples, and said:
   "Drink from this, all of you; this is my blood of the new
      covenant,
   poured out for you and for many for the forgiveness of sins.
Do this, as often as you drink it, in remembrance of me."

And so, in remembrance of these your mighty acts in Jesus
   Christ,
   we offer ourselves in praise and thanksgiving

releasing our shame in union with Christ's offering for us,
as we proclaim the mystery of faith.
Christ has died; Christ is risen; Christ will come again.

Pour out your Holy Spirit on each of us gathered here and these
gifts of bread and juice,
that in the sharing of your life-giving bread and cup of
salvation,
we will know true communion with you and each other.
Move in us so we are awake in each moment and experience
the abundant life you offer.
Make us aware of our guilt and shame and compassionately
transform us with grace.
Bring us alive with your Spirit, so we can authentically listen and
offer empathy to others.
Abide in us, so we will have strength and peace to be powerful
forces of love in the world.
Allow us to arise in the power of your resurrection fully alive to
our purpose and knowing eternal hope.
Through this communion, help us know our worth and feel in
our souls how we truly belong.
Thank you for this incredible invitation to experience your love
and grace.
We praise you and look forward to sharing this experience with
all your people
as we feast at your table forever.
Through Christ, with Christ, in Christ, in the unity of the Holy
Spirit,
all honor and glory is yours, almighty God, now and forever.
Amen.[16]

INTERFAITH BLESSING AND INSTRUCTIONS FOR SHARING

Unison prayer: God, awaken us to the abundance of blessings you give us through the earth's offering of grapes and bread. In this circle of sharing, make us aware how our guilt and shame are transformed by grace and acceptance. Bring us alive, so we can authentically listen and offer empathy to others. Abide in us, so we will have strength and peace to be powerful forces of love in the world. After our sharing, help us arise with purpose and hope. Through this sharing help us know our worth and feel in our souls how we truly belong. Amen.

As you share the grapes and bread with the person to your left in the circle, here are some examples of words you can offer:

- "[Insert Person's Name], I offer you the love and peace of God."
- "[Insert Person's Name], this is a gift of grace and connection from God."

Abide Reflection

Take a few moments to reflect on your experience of receiving and sharing communion in light of your work regarding shame. Write anything that comes to mind, and record how you feel in your body about this experience.

_____

_____

_____

_____

_____

_____

ARISE

Today we learned about overcoming shame and experiencing communion. Use the practices to continue overcoming shame and seeking connection to yourself, God, and others.

Home Practices for This Week

1. Practice your Awake meditation each day for 3 minutes.

2. Reread the Abide spiritual practice and focus on what communion means to you for 3 minutes each day.

3. Check in with your partner at least twice this week.

4. Keep track of your efforts in the journal area that follows. For example, "Day 1 [date], I practiced the Awake and Abide practices." Then record your thoughts, emotions, and any physical sensations you notice. Keep in mind that there is no wrong answer.

_____

_____

_____

_____

_____

_____

_____

_____

_____

_____

_____

_____

_____

_____

_____

_____

_____

Closing Blessing

At the end of each session, we will share this unison blessing.

We are awakening to abundant life.
We are becoming aware of our worth and belonging.
We are becoming alive to our senses, thoughts, and emotions.
We are abiding in the love and grace of God.
We arise now to live a life as connected, whole people.

CONNECTING TO CREATION

This week we will focus on awakening to the power of our connection to nature. Let's check in regarding your practices before we dig in this week.

- Look over your journal. How did the practices go?
- Is it becoming easier to sit with your thoughts and emotions?

AWAKE

When was the last time you sat appreciating the rustling of green, lush leaves with the backdrop of an indigo sky? The sun bathed your face in warmth and the wind caressed your face. Maybe there was a day when you went outside after a rain to smell the clean air while counting the earthworms pushed to the surface. A puddle of water called to you to jump and splash. A mud pie needed to be made and squished through your fingers. What about an evening outside when you glimpsed the first star appearing at dusk and enjoyed the fading light as you waited for the flash of a firefly to chase? Even better, you stayed still so the fireflies came close and you were surrounded by their light under the glow of starlight.

Or perhaps you lay on your back and made a snow angel in freshly fallen snow. Simple moments such as these are gifts from our Creator God.

In the beginning, God placed the earth neither too far nor too close to the sun to perfectly sustain life. Then God created us along with plants and animals and gave us the role of gardener, steward of the planet. For some, this will literally mean using their hands to dig in the earth, planting the seed and nurturing the growth of food and flowers. For all, it means connecting to the seasons, praying for the farmers, not using more resources than we need, and holding awe in our hearts for the miracle of the cycle of life. Yet, with modern grocery stores and transportation, we are disconnected from how our food is raised and the growing seasons. In our busyness, we consume the earth's resources with little thought and appreciation. We can walk from our dorms or apartments to class with our ear buds in, without noticing the sun, the trees, the clouds, or the bird's chirp of greeting. Connecting to nature takes intentionality, but it is another key to wholeness.

Awake Exercise

Our Awake exercise is slightly different this week. As we expand our watchfulness to nature, listen to or read "Canticle of Brother Sun and Sister Moon" by St. Francis of Assisi. Then take some time in centering prayer to focus on your awe of God's creation. The practice of centering prayer is an invitation to intentionally focus on God's presence in and around you for a time. Here are some simple instructions for centering prayer:

Centering Prayer Instructions

1. Listen to the audio track of the Canticle of St. Francis. This track can be found at www.theawakenedlife.info.

2. Pick a sacred word from this text to bring you back into focus, such as *light, peace, cherish* . . .

3. Sit comfortably with eyes closed and your mind open to God.

4. When your mind begins to wander and thoughts begin to form, say your sacred word and gently return to focusing.

5. After the centering prayer time is over, take a few moments to register any thoughts, emotions, or sensations in your body that you experienced during the prayer.

Audio Track 8: "Canticle of Brother Sun and Sister Moon" by St. Francis of Assisi—Dr. Sarah Bollinger, LCSW

Listen to the audio track of "Canticle of Brother Sun and Sister Moon" by St. Frances of Assisi, found at www.theawakenedlife.info, or read the text below.

> Most High, all-powerful, all-good Lord, All praise is Yours, all glory, all honor and all blessings.
> To you alone, Most High, do they belong, and no mortal lips are worthy to pronounce Your Name.
>
> Praised be You my Lord with all Your creatures,
> especially Sir Brother Sun,
> Who is the day through whom You give us light.
> And he is beautiful and radiant with great splendor,
> Of You Most High, he bears the likeness.
>
> Praised be You, my Lord, through Sister Moon and the stars,
> In the heavens you have made them bright, precious and fair.
>
> Praised be You, my Lord, through Brothers Wind and Air,
> And fair and stormy, all weather's moods,
> by which You cherish all that You have made.
>
> Praised be You my Lord through Sister Water,
> So useful, humble, precious and pure.

Praised be You my Lord through Brother Fire,
through whom You light the night and he is beautiful and
      playful and robust and strong.
Praised be You my Lord through our Sister,
Mother Earth
who sustains and governs us,
producing varied fruits with colored flowers and herbs.

Praise be You my Lord through those who grant pardon for love
      of You and bear sickness and trial.
Blessed are those who endure in peace, By You Most High,
      they will be crowned.

Praised be You, my Lord through Sister Death,
from whom no-one living can escape. Woe to those who die in
      mortal sin! Blessed are they She finds doing Your Will.

No second death can do them harm. Praise and bless
      my Lord and give Him thanks,
And serve Him with great humility.

Awake Prayer

Let's say this prayer together as we end the exercise:

*God, help me stay connected to my sense of awe for creation. In this
we pray, amen.*

Group Check-In

- How did it feel to listen to the "Canticle of Brother Sun and Sister
  Moon"?
- Did listening to this canticle before the centering prayer help you cen-
  ter on your awe of nature?

- Why did you pick your centering word, and did it help you stay focused?

AWARE

No longer do we rise with the sun and lie down when the sun sets. With the Industrial Revolution and the continuing creation of new and advancing technology, we increasingly work less outside. These advances often make life easier and expand our ability to learn, yet it is taking a toll on our well-being. We were created to connect to the rhythms of the earth: the rising and setting of the sun, and the seasons.

Not surprisingly, scientific research shows time in nature has a positive impact on physical, emotional, and spiritual well-being. "According to the best available evidence, nature contact offers considerable promise in addressing a range of health challenges, including many, such as obesity, cardiovascular disease, depression, and anxiety, that are public health priorities. Contact with nature offers promise both as prevention and as treatment across the life course."[17] Yet, even though we hear these kinds of reports about the importance of time in nature, the time we spend outside is not increasing. Research experts note that "total media consumption" is on the rise, with the average per day among adults being 10 hours and 39 minutes per day among adults and rising.[18] Research also demonstrates that park visitation, camping, hunting, fishing, and children playing outdoors have all declined substantially over recent decades.[19]

Aware Journaling

Before we spend some time outside, take a few moments to journal your answers to the following questions:

1. Has there been a time when you felt you were in your right place in the world? Where was that?

2. Have you experienced a sense of connection with God in the natural world?

3. How and where did you experience this connection to God in creation?

4. Do you miss having time outside? If so, what keeps you from being outside?

5. Where do you sense there is brokenness in our human-earth connection?

ALIVE

"But ask the animals, and they will teach you;
the birds of the air, and they will tell you; ask
the plants of the earth, and they will teach
you; and the fish of the sea will declare to
you. Who among all these does not know
that the hand of the LORD has done this?
In his hand is the life of every living thing
and the breath of every human being."

JOB 12:7-10, NRSV

Prayer Walk Instructions

Since this week the focus is on nature, our goal is to spend a period of time outside.

As you walk you are invited to do the following:

- Set a timer for 15 minutes on your phone, but then please put it away to give nature your focus.
- If your mind wanders, use your mindfulness practices to bring your-self gently back into focus without judgment.
- Feel and silently express gratitude for what you see and hear.
- Pray that abundant life is experienced by all you encounter.
- Pray for connection and appreciation for the world around you.
- As a final act of wakefulness, take your shoes off and feel grounded in the earth solidly supporting you, if the weather is nice. Sit in a comfortable place and pick one living organism: for example, a leaf, a blade of grass, a bug, or tree bark. Then spend your last 5-10 minutes

looking at it with a loving gaze. Open yourself to what God is revealing through this small part of creation.

- Come back to the group to share your experience.

> "We have so many reasons to be happy. The earth is filled with love for us, and patience. Whenever she sees us suffering, she will protect us. With the earth as a refuge, we need not be afraid of anything, even dying. Walking mindfully on the earth, we are nourished by the trees, the bushes, the flowers, and the sunshine. Touching the earth is a very deep practice that can restore our peace and our joy."
>
> **THICH NHAT HANH**

Group Conversation

Share your reflections about the prayer walk with the larger group by working through these questions.

- What happened in your body as you experienced the outdoors? What did you notice?
- Was this practice uncomfortable?

 ΛBIDE

Fasting has been passed down through many faith traditions for countless generations. During Ramadan, Muslims use fasting as a practice of faithfulness. They observe the fast from dawn until dusk, and refrain from food, drink, and immoral behavior. In the Judeo-Christian tradition, fasting is the practice of going without food for a certain amount of time to focus on our dependence on God. Jesus practiced fasting to prepare for his ministry and to seek God's wisdom, and he invites his followers to participate in this type of prayerful watchfulness for God's movement in the world. In Methodism, founder "John Wesley practiced a weekly fast from sundown on Thursday to sundown on Friday. He refrained from eating food while taking water and tea during the day. On Friday evening, he broke the fast with a light meal (broth, bread, and water or tea). During the fast Wesley spent much of the time in prayer and reading Scripture."[20] You are invited this week to do a Wesleyan fast. We do acknowledge not all people can or should participate in a fast due to health conditions. If it is appropriate for your body to undertake a fast, consider spending the time you would normally spend on meal preparation and eating by being outside instead, appreciating nature and praying. If you want an idea of how to spend your time, you can repeat the Alive walking prayer from this week.

"Fasting must forever center on God. . . . More than any other single discipline, fasting reveals the things that control us. This is a wonderful benefit to the true disciple who longs to be transformed into the image of Jesus Christ. We cover up what is inside us with food and other good things, but in fasting, these things surface."

RICHARD ROHR

Food Fast Reflections

After your food fast, pause to reflect on these questions:

- How does hunger feel in your body?
- What thoughts and feelings come to mind when you fast?
- What does this time teach you about your dependence on God and God's creation?
- How can this bring you closer to people who experience hunger on a daily basis?
- What temptations try to draw you away from focusing on God's presence in the moments of your fasting?

Technology "Fast" Reflections

On other days or in place of a food fast, consider "fasting" from technology for an hour a day. Again, spend that time outside, with an openness to God's activity in you and around you in nature. Each day, take a few moments to process what this focused time with nature does in your body, mind, and spirit. Pause after your technology fast to reflect on these questions:

- How did your desire for technology feel in your body?
- What thoughts and feelings come to mind when you abstain from technology?
- What did you see, smell, and hear when you set your technology aside to be present outside?
- How did this bring you closer to God?
- Did you experience wonder and awe in regard to something you saw in nature?
- What things tempted you to shift your focus from God's presence in nature?

Today we learned about the power of connecting to nature. Use the home practices to continue increasing your awareness about the natural environment and how it impacts your well-being.

During next week's session, you will also be invited to prepare and eat a meal together. Before you leave today, your group leader will help your group create a plan for the meal and will ask each of you to participate.

Home Practices for This Week

1. Practice your Awake centering prayer each day for 3 minutes.

2. Try the Abide spiritual tradition (fasting practice) each day. If you are going to practice the food fast, we recommend fasting the two meals before we meet again. We will break our fast together with a shared meal. Find the reflection questions for the fast during the week in the Abide section.

3. Check in with your partner at least twice this week.

4. Keep track of your efforts in the journal area that follows. For example, "Day 1 [date], I practiced the Awake and Abide practices." Then record your thoughts, emotions, and any physical sensations you notice. Keep in mind that there is no wrong answer.

Closing Blessing

At the end of each session we will share this unison blessing.

We are awakening to abundant life.
We are becoming aware of our worth and belonging.
We are becoming alive to our senses, thoughts, and emotions.
We are abiding in the love and grace of God.
We arise now to live a life as connected, whole people.

CONNECTING TO CREATION

SHARING A MEAL OF INTENTION

This week, we will focus on experiencing God through our connections with self, others, and creation in the sharing of a meal, but first let's check in regarding your mindfulness and fasting practice.

- How did your practices go this week?
- Did you take any nature walks?
- Did you practice fasting from food and/or technology?
- How did it go, and what insights did you learn about yourself?

AWAKE

For weeks, we have been working to quiet our minds and limit distractions, experiencing God through our connections with self, others, and nature. As we seek wholeness and salvation together, the meal we are going to share is a beautiful way of bringing all of our work together. God's presence in the making, preparing, and sharing of a meal provides an opportunity to experience the sacred. Meals give us a glimpse of heaven. We find heaven here, in moments of perfected love of God, creation, self, and others. As we come together for a meal, creation offers us nourishment, others bless us with their presence, we share ourselves in conversation, and God binds us all together in love.

Throughout different cultures, people are awake to the powerful connectedness of a shared meal. The Lakota Sioux people have a beautiful prayer, "Mitakuye Oyasin," celebrating God's creation through our connection to minerals, plants, animals, humans, and Spirit.

> "You are all my relations,
> my relatives, without whom
> I would not live."
>
> **LAKOTA SIOUX PRAYER**

We can glean so much wisdom from our indigenous brothers and sisters about giving thanks for the blessings of creation and our interconnectedness. They remind us that when the earth thrives, we thrive, and when the earth hurts, so do we.

The Judeo-Christian faith tradition awakens us to the power of meals for relationship building and transformation. Meals are experiences of radical hospitality and love. At a meal, there is respect and care not only for friends but for all who join around the table. Jesus revealed God's intention for meals by inviting himself to a greedy tax collector's house and restoring that man to his community (Luke 19:1-10). At a prestigious dinner party, Jesus audaciously welcomed and allowed a "sinful woman" to anoint his feet with oil (Luke 7:36-37, CEV). He blessed her with healing and hope. Another time, thousands were gathered for his teachings, and at mealtime the disciples wanted Jesus to send the people away to feed themselves. Yet Jesus invited a miraculous sharing, and all were fed to the point of full bellies and souls (Matthew 16:13-21; Mark 6:30-44). Powerful things happen at meals. Lives are shared and connected by the simple yet profound act of breaking bread together as we open to God's possibilities for our lives.

> "Glance at the sun. See the moon and the stars. Gaze at the beauty of earth's greenings. Now, think. What delight God gives to humankind with all these things. All nature is at the disposal of humankind. We are to work with it. For without we cannot survive."
>
> **HILDEGARD OF BINGEN**

AWARE

In our fast-food culture, the preparing and sharing of meals often goes missing. A Nutrisystem commissioned survey of two thousand people revealed "35 percent of those surveyed aged 18 to 25 feel they need to have their phone for every meal that they eat." They also estimate one in three Americans "can't get through a meal without being on their phones."[21] This leads to disconnection from the people you are eating with as well as disconnection from your food. While distracted by their phones, people are more likely to chew less and overeat. To get the health benefits of shared meals, three things are crucial: putting down your phone, engaging in conversation, and being grateful for the meal in front of you. Practice these three things at mealtime as an additional step on your path to well-being.

To be truly grateful for the meal you are about to share as a group, be aware of the origin of the meal. Be grateful for those who tended the components of the meal before it arrived at the table, and be aware of how your food's production impacts the earth and others, both positively and negatively. Regardless of whether your meal is simple, such as apples, cheese and crackers, or a take-out pizza, or whether you are able to cook a full meal together, take some time to think about what it took to grow, process, and transport this meal.

Awareness Group Research and Discussion

Break out into small groups of two or three. Based on the meal your group will eat together, assign each group an ingredient to research. For example, if you are having pizza, research one of the ingredients—flour, tomatoes, cheese, or garlic—and its pathway to your table. Find out as much as you can about this item on the Internet using the questions in the following bulleted list. You have space for research notes below. Then report back to the group.

1. Where was this ingredient likely grown, and is it in season in our region right now?

2. What went into the growing and making of this ingredient?

3. How were people positively and negatively impacted by its growth or production to get it to our shared table?

4. How was the earth positively and negatively impacted by its growth or production to get it to our shared table?

5. What nutritional value does this ingredient offer our bodies?

6. How does knowing these details make you more grateful for the food we are about to eat?

_____

_____

_____

_____

_____

_____

_____

_____

_____

_____

_____

_____

_____

ALIVE

Remember the Raisin Meditation in Week 3; this week we will use the same approach for our meal. In an effort to be fully present to our senses and the beauty of the food we are eating, for 10 minutes this meal will be eaten in silence. This is an effort to savor and express gratitude. Here are some things to be aware of to experience the most in this meal:

- Be silent for 10 minutes while eating.
- What do you smell, feel, taste, and experience with each bite?
- Make sure to chew each bite 30 times.
- Think back to our Aware section discussion; what process went into the making of this food?

- Take a moment to be thankful for each step of this process and all the people and natural resources needed to nourish your body in this moment.

Meal Conversation Starters

After the time of silence, share together in a meal conversation about the following questions:

1. How did it feel to eat in silence and truly stay present to your eating experience?

2. When you eat at the dining hall or in your apartment, how mindful are you of what the food does for your body, the people who grew and prepared it, and those who don't have sufficient food?

3. What were the meal practices as you were growing up? Did you eat together?

4. What kind of conversations did you have? Or, was the TV on during dinner?

5. What do you think should be a good example of eating together— what you experienced as a child, or something different?

6. What priorities or activities take precedence over eating together at meals?

7. What are the values behind how we eat, and how do they foster disconnection from creation and others?

8. What are practices you will incorporate into your life to show gratitude and thanksgiving over the food you eat?

ABIDE

Our Abide prayer practice is an Ignatian method of prayer provided by The Upper Room. It explains how to practice this method of prayer in the following way: "Think of the Ignatian Method of prayer—named after Ignatius of Loyola (1491–1556)—as a sort of virtual experience of the scripture where you read the scripture and then create in your mind a short film about what you read. In the Ignatian Method, you enter into the story so that you can learn more about and participate more fully in the mind, the heart, and the work of Christ."

Abide Practice Instructions

As you read the scripture, reflect on questions such as:

- What do I see and hear? What do I smell, taste, or touch?
- Who are the characters and what's going on with them?
- If I were in this movie, what role would I play?
- If I were Jesus in this story, what would I be thinking, feeling, saying?"[22]

Use this practice with the following scriptures and see where your imagination takes you. Please feel free to pick your own scriptures, and if you do not identify as Christian, you are invited to use this practice with writings from your faith tradition. Here are some suggested meal scriptures:

- Luke 9:12-17, Jesus feeds the multitudes
- Luke 7:36-50, Jesus welcomes a sinful woman to a meal
- Luke 14:16-24, the parable of the great dinner
- Luke 19:1-10, Jesus invites himself to dinner
- Psalm 23, God sets a table of abundant life

If you do not identify as Christian, please consider following the same practice with a sacred text about meals from your tradition or one of the following poems:

- "Perhaps the World Ends Here" by Joy Harjo:

  An excerpt: "The world begins at a kitchen table. No matter what, we must eat to live."

  The full poem can be found at: https://www.poetryfoundation.org /poems/49622/perhaps-the-world-ends-here.

- "The Potato" by Joseph Stroud

  An excerpt: "What matters to me most, was that farmer, alone on his hillside."

  The full poem can be found at: https://m.poets.org/poetsorg/poem /potato.

ARISE

Today, we awakened to experiencing God through our connections with self, others, and creation in the sharing of a meal. Use the home practices for staying awake to our interconnectedness.

Home Practices for This Week

1. Practice your Awake exercise (food mindfulness practice) one meal each day, working up to all meals.

2. Try the Abide spiritual tradition (Ignatian Method of Prayer) every day for 3 minutes.

3. Check in with your partner at least twice this week.

4. Keep track of your efforts in the journal area that follows. For example, "Day 1 [date], I practiced the Awake and Abide practices." Then record your thoughts, emotions, and any physical sensations you notice. Keep in mind that there is no wrong answer.

Closing Blessing

At the end of each session, we will share this unison blessing.

We are awakening to abundant life.
We are becoming aware of our worth and belonging.
We are becoming alive to our senses, thoughts, and emotions.
We are abiding in the love and grace of God.
We arise now to live a life as connected, whole people.

CLOSING

AWAKENING TO JOY

Welcome back to our final week together. Today, we will talk about how an awakened life is a joyful, grateful life. Let's start by checking in regarding our weekly practices one last time.

- Did you incorporate mindful eating into your week? How did it feel?
- How did practicing the Ignatian Prayer go for you?
- Did you learn anything new about yourself or God?

AWAKE

Our work together over the last seven weeks is just the beginning of an awakened, abundant life. You are building the skills to be fully awake to your feelings and thoughts, and how they live in your body. This means you can notice, feel, and listen to them, paying attention to how they impact your life. This conscious awareness will help you face criticism and disappointments with a sense of your own worth and prevent disconnection. This will build a life of connection, and these connections will strengthen you to face challenges and thrive.

In the Christian tradition, connection to the Spirit of God empowers a life of love, joy, peace, patience, kindness, goodness, faithfulness, gentleness, and self-control (Galatians 5:22-23, CEB). A life full of these things is resilient and perseveres through struggles.

Awake Exercise

One way we can begin to awaken to joy is to cultivate gratitude. Often we forget or simply take for granted all of the things in our lives that are causes for thankfulness. Being aware of these things takes some intention and practice. Mindfully engaging in a regular gratitude practice can help. Try this Gratitude Meditation as a group, and be curious about how the meditation feels for you.

> "Every day, think as you wake up: Today I am fortunate to have woken up. I am alive. I have a precious human life. I am not going to waste it. I am going to use all my energies to develop myself, to expand my heart out to others, to achieve enlightenment for the benefit of all beings."
>
> **THE DALAI LAMA**

Audio Track 9: Gratitude Meditation—Dr. Sarah Bollinger, LCSW

Listen to the audio track online at www.theawakenedlife.info. or have your leader read this aloud to the group.

Begin by finding some stillness. Sit upright in a comfortable, supported position, where your back and neck are straight but relaxed. If you feel comfortable, allow your eyes to gently close, or just maintain a soft gaze, focusing on a spot in front of you. Take a slow, deep breath to bring yourself into the present moment. As you gently bring your awareness to your breath, notice the inhalations and exhalations. Then take a few moments to scan your body, noticing any sensations of tension or stress, allowing the muscles to relax.

Now that your body, thoughts, and emotions are a bit more centered, begin to focus your awareness on the events, experiences, people, places, pets, or possessions for which you feel grateful. You might first recall that you already have several marvelous gifts available to you in this moment. Regardless of your circumstances, you are sharing in the gift of life right now. Take a moment to be grateful for your heartbeat. Notice how your heart feels beating in your chest, and take a moment to express thanks for the work that your heart does to pump life-giving blood throughout your body. Extend this with gratitude for your senses. Notice what you hear or smell or feel in the room, and be grateful for the gift of your senses.

Now take a moment to note all the things that make your life easier and more comfortable than previous generations. Maybe express gratitude for electricity, the ability to drive a car, the clean water that flows from your tap, and the roof that you have over your head. Now take a moment to thank all the people who have worked hard, many without knowing it, to make your life full. Cultivate gratitude for the farmers who grow your food, the postal workers who deliver your mail, those who work on servers to maintain our Internet services, and the teams who build our roads and highways. Now consider the people and pets in your personal sphere of influence, and extend thanks to each of the individuals that bring joy to your life.

As you finish this exercise, bring your awareness back to your breath. Notice if it has shifted at all during this meditation. Notice how your body is feeling at this moment. As you are ready, open your eyes.

Prayer

Let's say this prayer together as we end the exercise:

God, help me continue to be awake to your presence in all aspects of my life. In this we pray, amen.

Group Check-In

- How did it feel to participate in the Gratitude Meditation?
- Think back to the first time you did this exercise in Week 1. How is it the same and how is it different?
- Has this practice become part of your daily life?

> "'Thank you' is the best prayer that anyone could say. I say that one a lot. Thank you expresses extreme gratitude, humility, understanding."
>
> **ALICE WALKER**

AWARE

Spiritual disciplines and mindfulness only help reduce stress and foster well-being when they are practiced. All the mindful, meditative, and spiritual practices you have experienced during our time together help to train your mind to tolerate negativity, boredom, and anxiety. The practices offer calm in the storm of life by connecting you to God over and over through our relationships with self, others, and nature. Instead of sharing more science or more practices, let's use this time to stay awake and aware of what you have learned during our time together.

Aware Reflection

Take a few moments to look back at your notes from the last seven weeks. In the space provided by your leader, write the most powerful revelation or insight you carry with you from each week. After everyone is finished writing their takeaways, have a time of group sharing based on the following questions:

- What was most meaningful for you?
- What did someone else write that resonated with you?
- After all these weeks, what does abundant life mean to you now?

> "We need resilience and hope and a spirit that can carry us through the doubt and fear. We need to believe that we can effect change if we want to live and love with our whole hearts."
>
> **BRENÉ BROWN**

During this last Alive section, you are invited to practice gratitude for this group. Thankfulness is a cultivator of joy. This will help establish some strategies for making mindfulness and spiritual practices a part of your whole life.

Group Gratitude Exercise

One great joy is the time we have had together as a group. Gratitude is a powerful way to express our joy and appreciation for each other. To celebrate this, we are going to form gratitude circles. Create an inner and outer circle with even numbers of people; if necessary to form an even number, the group leader may join. The outer circle will move clockwise while the inner circle stays stationary. Each person in the pair will tell the person they face what they are grateful for about that person and/or how that person helped or inspired them over the eight weeks. This sharing will be limited to 3 minutes per pair. Keep going until everyone arrives back at their first pairing. When everyone returns to their seats, you may want to take a moment to write down some of the amazing things people shared about you.

_____

_____

_____

_____

_____

_____

_____

_____

_____

_____

"Joy collected over time, fuels resilience—ensuring we will have reservoirs of emotional strength when hard things do happen."

BRENÉ BROWN

Personal Exercise

To help you clarify what you want to take with you from this guide, we invite you to write yourself a letter. Your leader will check in with you at the beginning of the next semester and hand you or mail you your letter. This letter will further encourage you to make these life-giving practices a part of your life. Here are some ideas for what to share:

- Include any insights you have learned about yourself during these 8 weeks. How have you grown?
- List the practices you want to continue after this session.
- Make sure to write down some of the wonderful things people said to you during the gratitude circle time.
- Also, write what you are most thankful for regarding this experience and your life right now.

ABIDE

This final week, the traditional spiritual practice to explore is the Daily Examen. Ignatius of Loyola, a sixteenth-century cleric and theologian, created the Daily Examen. This is a practice of gratitude for God's presence and our connection to each other.

Examen Prayer Instructions

The Prayer of Examen is an awareness and gratitude prayer used to reflect on your day. It has been passed down through Christian generations as a practice to give God our attention, listen for God's direction, and cultivate a thankful attitude for all the moments in our lives. Here are some simple instructions for examining your day through prayer. Journaling your experience is often helpful, so there is room below to jot down any thoughts, feelings, and moments of gratitude and/or clarity from God about your life.[23]

1. Invite God's Presence: Take a few moments to invite the Holy Spirit to help you see where God was active in and working through you during the day.

2. Cultivate Gratitude: As you walk through your day in your mind, what are moments you are particularly thankful for and why?

3. Check Your Emotions: What emotions did you experience today? What are they teaching you about yourself?

4. Pick a Moment: Choose a scene from your day and pray about it with extra focus. Was there a moment in which you regretted your words, actions, or thoughts? Are forgiveness and reconnection needed? What about a moment that was life-giving? What does that reveal about your passions and what is truly important to you?

5. Look Forward: What is coming up in your life? Are there areas of your life in which you want to ask God for strength, direction, connection, and/or hope?

_____

_____

_____

_____

_____

_____

_____

_____

_____

_____

_____

_____

_____

"Rejoice always, pray without
ceasing, give thanks in all
circumstances; for this is the will
of God in Christ Jesus for you."

1 THESSALONIANS 5:16-18, NRSV

Today is the last day of this guide but only the beginning of an awakened life. We hope you carry all the practices with you and use them when the struggles of life come. Being able to draw on your mindful and spiritual practices will result in peace and joy to increasingly be your experience.

Home Practices for This Week and Beyond

1. Practice being awake every day through the Awake and Abide section exercises you learned in this group. This will keep you connected to God, yourself, others, and nature.

2. Cultivate self-compassion and gratitude.

3. Keep connected to your partner and others in the group.

4. Continue to journal your emotions and thoughts, the way they impact your body, mind, and spirit. Wholeness is at your fingertips.

Closing Blessing

Carry this blessing with you into your awakened life.

We are awakening to abundant life.
We are becoming aware of our worth and belonging.
We are becoming alive to our senses, thoughts, and emotions.
We are abiding in the love and grace of God.
We arise now to live a life as connected, whole people.

THE AWAKENED LIFE

AN 8-WEEK GUIDE
TO STUDENT WELL-BEING

LEADER GUIDE

PREFACE

Welcome to *The Awakened Life Leader Guide*. Our hope is that this small-group curriculum provides tools and practices that will help you empower students to live a more abundant life.

WHY WE CREATED THIS CURRICULUM

This curriculum was created as a response to a direct call from campus ministers and chaplains. The General Board of Higher Education and Ministry (GBHEM) recently conducted an assessment that surveyed campus ministers and university chaplains across the United Methodist connection. The findings from this assessment indicated that chaplains and campus ministers are facing declining emotional, mental, and spiritual health among college students and are spending a majority of their time helping students cope with these issues. Our findings were verified by research that documents increasing rates of depression, anxiety, and other mental health issues specifically among young adults. Furthermore, college chaplains and ministers asserted that while this is an ever-increasing area of concern in their ministry, they rarely have the training and resources available to adequately address these concerns. In response to this need, GBHEM assembled a team of United Methodist experts and leaders to respond to this call, with the goal of providing a concrete resource to use with students.

WHAT THIS INITIATIVE IS AND WHAT IT IS NOT

The end result of this response to the need expressed by campus ministers and chaplains is what you hold in your hands: an eight-week curriculum meant to guide students through practices that build resiliency, teach psychosocial skills, and foster emotional and spiritual well-being.

This is not a traditional Bible study. While we engage scripture and talk about well-being from a United Methodist theological lens, this is not a scriptural study of well-being.

In the same vein, this is not a clinical intervention. We do not intend for this to be a replacement for mental health treatment or therapy. Referral to necessary mental health resources is the correct response to a mental health crisis or symptoms that could lead to a diagnosis of mental illness.

With that said, this is a resource to equip those who are working on the front lines with students in nonclinical roles; it is designed for those who provide spiritual and emotional care to students but who are not counselors or therapists. The scope of this project focuses on equipping ministers and chaplains to assist students with nonclinical resiliency training and psychosocial skill building, with the goal of improving well-being. Furthermore, this resource leans on the fact that our faith can help us in this task. This project was conceptualized to respond to nonclinical issues of well-being among students, with an intentional focus on using our faith tradition and practices to inform this work.

Mindfulness

Part of the way we address student well-being is through using mindfulness techniques. We know that mindfulness practices including meditation contribute to improved mood, concentration, and relationships. Our faith tradition also has a lot to add to the conversation around mindfulness, and we share rich contemplative practices that point to this truth. With this knowledge in mind, we approach this curriculum with the intention of teaching students to be more present and able to navigate emotional disturbance with presence of mind.

Mindfulness and Christianity

Christianity and mindfulness go hand in hand. For those who are interested in the connection between the two, Amy Oden's book *Right Here, Right Now*[24] is a wonderful resource.

HOW THIS GUIDE WORKS

This curriculum walks through eight weeks of well-being practices and reflections. Each weekly session is about an hour and a half long and includes various practices and experiences that you will walk through as a group. Many of these practices involve various prayer and meditation techniques, coupled with discussion and journaling. While there are set tasks to complete, plan to give your students sufficient space and time to work through the content. It's OK to make this time unique to your style and tailor it to suit the participants of your group. Each week contains key practices that are central to the weekly theme, and these can be guideposts for how you choose to lead each session. If you don't make it through every activity or discussion, that is perfectly all right.

Please be aware that this curriculum works best when conducted as a "closed group." In other words, having an expectation that participants will attend consistently and the same group members will be attending the sessions each week is ideal. While much of this guide can be adapted for other settings, consistency and regular attendance is helpful in seeing lasting change among group members. As the leader of this group, it will also be helpful for you to read the weekly instructions in this guide in preparation for each session. While there isn't extensive preparation before each session, there are some logistics to be aware of as you plan for the weekly content.

The Awakened Life is organized into three central components. Using systems theory as its framework, these components help students connect deeply with ever-increasing circles of wholeness at work in and through them. We are conceptualizing wholeness in three central areas: connection to self and the work of the divine within, connection to others in deep relationship, and connection to creation. The weeks start with an introductory week, then follow this flow: two weeks understanding our relationship with ourselves, two weeks focusing on deepening our relationships with others, two weeks connecting with nature, and, finally, a closing session in week 8. A brief outline of the full student guide follows:

Week 1. Introduction to the Awakened Life

Week 2. Connecting to Self: Noticing Thoughts

Week 3. Connecting to Self: Being Present in the Body

Week 4. Connecting to Others: Working through Loneliness

Week 5. Connecting to Others: Working through Shame

Week 6. Connecting to Creation: Experiencing Awe of Nature

Week 7. Connecting to Creation: Sharing a Meal of Intention

Week 8. Closing: Awakening to Joy

Weekly Content

Each week's session is divided into a series of sections. The sections will be consistent across all weeks and help to establish a rhythm from week to week. The different sections are as follows:

Awake: Sessions will begin with an introductory section in which possibilities for wholeness will be explored as a group. This is the students' call to wake up, join in, and participate in this work each week. The Awake section is inspired by a moment in Jesus's life when he was seeking connection and support from his friends in moments of struggle. Three times he found them asleep in the Garden of Gethsemane during his most critical moment of need and unable to join with him in prayer. How often are we asleep to what God is doing in our midst?

Aware: From awakening we will move into a greater awareness about the realities of our world. This section will contain information, research, and stories about the weekly topic to help personalize the content. This Aware section is inspired by our desire not to be conformed to this distracted and anxious world. We will be aware of how our minds are being transformed and opened to experience God's perfect goodness and wholeness.

Alive: Becoming alive involves true engagement. This section will contain group discussions and activities to help students embody and bring to life the topics at hand. This section is inspired by the Judeo-Christian creation story, when God breathes life into humanity. We will breathe, think, speak, and move intimately connected to self, others, and nature.

Abide: This section will revisit many of our inherited, Christian spiritual practices and connect students with God at work in themselves, in their relationships, and in the world. This section was inspired by Jesus's invitation to remain in his love. Abiding is a deep sense of connection and security in this experience. If students do not identify as Christian, there are a number of suggested ways to adapt this material.

Arise: After the group session ends, the Arise section offers home practices and assignments that students should visit between sessions, so they can go out into the world, equipped and energized to engage in new ways. This section was inspired by the resurrection of Jesus Christ, and this incredible power of bringing life out of death is available to us. Darkness cannot overcome the light, and you can carry this hope with you during this group study and beyond.

A Word about Practicing at Home

Each week will offer a series of practices the students will be asked to do between sessions. These are short, manageable exercises that are simple and should be completed each day. We invite students to journal each day to track their experiences. There is space within the student guide to write, or students are free to use their own personal journals. There is not a right or wrong way to do the practices; the important thing is that they begin and keep at it. We also highly recommend that students hold one another accountable for completing the assignments. We advise assigning partners who check in on each other from week to week. This increases accountability and cohesiveness in the group. As the group leader, it's important for you to model this to the group and establish your own rhythm of practice as well. Skill building and self-awareness take time, and regular practice is encouraged to bring about lasting change.

Things to Plan For

While most of this curriculum will not require a lot of preparation before sessions, there are a few things to be aware of as you begin.

- Each week begins with some preparation notes for you as the leader, to notify you about any special requirements for that session. Make sure to read the leader guide before your group meets each week to be ready in advance.

- All videos, audio tracks, and important links are located on The Awakened Life website at www.theawakenedlife.info. Feel free to share this website with your students so they can practice on their own.

- This process will require intentionality in terms of space and time. You might want to think about setting up the room in a way that is conducive to deeper "heart and soul work." You might think about scents, sounds, sights, and movements that would foster a safe, peaceful, and contemplative atmosphere.

- Students will need their workbooks each week and a pen for reflection. They also may want to bring their own journals to use alongside the workbook if they need more space to write.

- There might be periods of silence and time for reflection as students are invited to talk and journal about difficult topics. You can let your students know in advance that this is OK. Silence can be a welcomed guest in the process.

- Certain topics that you will discuss may be difficult for some students or trigger strong memories and reactions. Let students know they can sit with difficult emotions. It is equally important to know when to refer a student out to a mental health professional for additional work on issues that arise.

- Week 7 involves preparing a meal together as a practice of intentionality. Make necessary arrangements as you see fit, and make sure that each student has a role.

- Week 8 suggests giving each student a token of course completion as an optional symbol of your time together. Think ahead about this, and preorder or prepare anything that you might need for this experience. If you decide to give a picture of the group as your token, make sure to take this a few weeks in advance and print out copies.

Doing Your Own Work

We are firm believers in the idea that you can only teach the things you know. One of the most challenging aspects of this curriculum is that it requires you, as the leader, to model and practice mindfulness and well-being alongside your students. This means that you will need to be actively engaged in your own "heart and soul work."

There will be opportunities to share from your own life, and speaking from a place of depth is critical. We encourage you to share the ways you have awakened to your own life. Along these lines, it is strongly suggested that you attend our leaders' training retreat before facilitating a group and using this curriculum. During this retreat, you will learn about this material and be introduced to many of the practices. Most important, you will also be provided space to do the "heart and soul" work we mentioned earlier. Please reach out to us for more information about these retreats if you are interested in using this guide.

BLESSINGS ON THE JOURNEY

Our hope for you and your group is that this process brings about new insight, growth, hope, and ultimately well-being. We encourage you, as the leader on this journey, to be curious, open, and present to a process that can bring about great transformation. May you be filled with grace, and may you model what it means to live the awakened life in a world so full of sleepers.

INTRODUCTION TO THE AWAKENED LIFE

PREPARATION FOR THIS SESSION

For this session you will need the following things:

- **Internet access and a screen.** The Awake section asks students to stream a video that is available on The Awakened Life website. The video is called *Abundant Life* with Dr. Amy Oden. You can show this video to the whole group on a large screen or have the students watch the video on their phones in small groups if this is easier. You can also use the Internet to stream an audio track of the opening meditation in the Awake section. All videos, audio tracks, and important links are located at: www.theawakenedlife.info.

- **Whiteboard, chalkboard, or large Post-it Notes and markers**. Together you will create a covenant and set the stage for these upcoming eight weeks. Students will spend time brainstorming together about the types of guidelines that would help to make them safe and successful in this group.

- **Student partners.** To hold each other accountable, you may want to assign everyone a partner. These partners should be the same throughout the eight weeks. Partners will check in with each other about their weekly home practices and help each other complete these tasks.

(20–25 minutes)

The opening section of Week 1 introduces students to the idea of well-being and invites them to begin a journey of awakening to abundant life. During this introductory session, the leader will introduce terms and the group will get to know one another for the first time in this small group setting.

Read the opening paragraphs aloud to help with this process. The leader may want to share their own story about waking up to their own lives as a concrete example for students.

Preparation note: There is a short accompanying video and an audio track in this section that are both available to stream online. The video is called *Abundant Life* and the meditation is called "Opening Meditation"; both are available here: www.theawakenedlife.info.

This video is designed to prompt discussion about abundant life and provide an opening for conversation. After you watch the video as a group, allow students time to break out into pairs or triads to have some time for conversation and getting to know one another. Make sure that students know to listen closely to one another.

After discussion and the icebreaker, we invite you to move into the first group activity. This is a very short opening meditation exercise that will introduce students to the practice of quieting their hearts and minds. It is available to be streamed online, or you can read it aloud from the student guide. Be aware that for those who are doing this for the first time, this exercise may be extremely difficult. It may even be difficult for you as the leader. Let students know to be patient with themselves and reinforce that it's OK if this is difficult. You are also invited to share your experience of learning this practice. What was it like for you when you first tried this mindfulness exercise? After the mindfulness activity, allow students time to discuss this experience.

AWARE

(5 minutes)

This section will be brief, simply explaining some statistics about well-being and starting the conversation about cultivating strategies for change. As the leader, you can read this information out loud and see if anyone has questions.

ALIVE

(25–35 minutes)

Guide to Making a Covenant: The ROPES Exercise

As the group begins, establish boundaries and guidelines to set the stage for the work that you will do together. Dedicate time to this activity, and make it a collaborative process. The group process works by cultivating openness and vulnerability, and we invite you to explore ideas such as consistency, commitment, confidentiality, and accountability to clearly lay out the group's expectations of one another. Following is one example of an activity that can help a group create guidelines by consensus.

You can use this exercise to help you and your students come up with boundaries together.

Preparation Note: This activity will require the whiteboard or large Post-it Notes and markers.

- Write the words "Group Covenant" on the top of the large piece of paper or whiteboard. Then write the word "ROPES" vertically along the left-hand side.

- Explain that, like a safety net, the ROPES will serve as mutually agreed-upon guidelines to which everyone will adhere during your time together. Ropes can bind people together and connect people. On the flip side, if ropes are too tight, they can trip people up or even strangle them. What kind of rope is needed for the group to keep itself bound together and safe for all members?

- Elicit words from the students (related to group covenant) that begin with each of the letters of the word *ROPES*. Ask the students to explain why they have recommended a word and what it means to them. For example, *R*: respect, responsibility; *O*: openness, ownership; and so forth. Add your own suggestions.

- Ask for a general consensus about which guidelines are chosen.

- Record the covenant. Have students sign the covenant as evidence of their commitment. Copy the list and bring it to each session for the duration of the group, or make copies to give to each member of the group. You can post your ROPES on the wall as a reminder of the covenant you have made to one another for these eight weeks.

- Periodically, have the group take a moment to evaluate whether the group covenant established at the beginning of the semester is being followed and whether it works for the group. ROPES can be edited and changed to accommodate the group.

Preparation note: Commitment to home practices outside of the group will be an important piece. Bring this up with your students as you create your covenant. Decide to put students into pairs or triads for accountability.

Group Discussion Notes

Once the covenant is created, transition the group into a time of discussion about well-being. You may want to start this with a time of individual journaling or reflection, followed by larger group discussion.

(15–20 minutes)

Students will be asked to learn about and practice lectio divina, which is described in the student guide. In preparation, help set up a quiet space. Once you introduce the practice and answer any questions students might have, allow students to spread out and take time to explore this ancient practice.

(10 minutes)

Having a closing ritual will be important for each session. At this point, take time to reinforce the weekly practices, and make sure students know you will be revisiting these each week. Encourage the students to journal each time they complete their home practices. Practicing at home and journaling will be a critical component of each week and should be completed between sessions. Once again, students should be encouraged to find an accountability partner before they leave the first session. Together, read the closing blessing, which will be the same each week.

CONNECTING TO
SELF

NOTICING THOUGHTS

PREPARATION FOR THIS SESSION

For this session you will need the following things:

- **Internet access.** The Awake section asks students to find a specific poem online and read it aloud together in the group. You can also use the Internet to stream an audio track of the "Awareness Meditation," which is found in the Awake section. All videos, audio tracks, and important links are located at: www.theawakenedlife.info.
- **Journal and pens.** Students will be asked to journal about certain topics that are covered during this session. This workbook provides some space for journaling; however, students are also invited to bring their own journals. Pens or pencils will also be needed.

(20–25 minutes)

It might be helpful to begin this session by reviewing some of the important things that you discussed last week. After an introductory welcome or prayer, review the ROPES exercise and reiterate any important guidelines that the group created during Week 1 before you begin. Also review the home practices and see what the students practiced and observed about themselves. Continue to encourage them to check in with their partners and continue to practice.

The content of Week 2 begins to explore well-being from the inside out. This week's session talks about our relationship with our minds and how to practice quieting our thoughts to tune in to what God is doing deep within us. The Awake section teaches students a little bit about their relationship with their thoughts.

The first exercise in this section is based on a poem entitled "The Summer Day" by Mary Oliver, which can be located at www.loc.gov/poetry/180/133.html.

Preparation note: Pull up this poem and read it aloud to the group.

The focus of this poem is attention to and appreciation of the present moment. Once the poem is read, walk the students through the short "Awareness Meditation." You can use the audio track or read from the student guide. As they sit through this meditative practice, have the students simply notice their thoughts without judgment. A conversation about this practice after the meditation is recommended.

AWARE

(10–15 minutes)

This section offers a teaching moment. As the leader, take a few minutes to educate your students about the various negative thought patterns that can demand our attention by reading the Aware section out loud to the group. Ask students to journal about any of these thought patterns they have experienced in their own lives. Bringing awareness to these patterns can bring about new insight.

ALIVE

(20–30 minutes)

Group Exercise and Activity

The case study provides a simple example of the negative types of thinking outlined in the Aware section. It will be helpful to read through the story; brainstorm together about the negative thought patterns the students notice. Following this example, have students reflect on their own experiences with negative thought patterns and share any of their journal reflections they feel comfortable sharing with the group.

Self-Compassion

A critical component in this section is pausing to teach the students about the importance of self-compassion. When students begin learning the practice of quieting their minds, inevitably they will be distracted. This is completely expected and a typical part of the process. Distractions and negative thought patterns are a part of life. The important thing is how students talk to themselves about these distractions. Self-compassion is essential to the way we talk to ourselves when these thought patterns occur. The poem by Rumi can be read aloud and discussed to concretize these ideas of self-compassion.

 ABIDE

(10–15 minutes)

The "Practice of the Presence of God" is explained in detail in the student guide.

 ARISE

(10 minutes)

As you leave the session, reiterate to the students the importance of doing the practices at home, and walk them through keeping a journal. You might want to answer any questions they have from last week before ending your time together. This week also adds the opportunity to practice self-compassion. Notice when the students speak harshly to themselves, and prompt them to be mindful of this and to change such dialogue. Say the closing blessing together as you prepare to leave.

CONNECTING TO
SELF

BEING PRESENT IN THE BODY

PREPARATION FOR THIS SESSION

For this session you will need the following things:

- **Internet access.** You can use the Internet to stream an audio track of the Raisin Meditation in the Awake section and the Christian mindfulness practice in the Abide section. All videos, audio tracks, and important links are located at: www.theawakenedlife.info.

- **Raisins or dried fruit**. Any small piece of food will do. Small pieces of chocolate will work well too.

- **Journal and pens**. Students will be asked to journal about certain topics that are covered during this session. This workbook provides some space for journaling; however, students who need more space are invited to bring their own journals. Pens or pencils will also be needed.

AWAKE

(20–25 minutes)

Begin this session by checking in regarding the home practices. This will be a weekly routine and should be reiterated at each session. Take time to allow students to reflect on their practices and see what they noticed. You may also want to follow up on the covenant established during the first week to reiterate the importance of cultivating safety, honesty, and vulnerability.

Preparation note: You will be leading the students through a guided meditation that helps them focus on their senses. The Raisin Meditation can be done with any small piece of food. A raisin works well, but you can use any dried or fresh fruit, nuts, or even a small piece of chocolate. Whichever item you choose to use, have this on hand before the session begins.

Have students share in the large group about their experience with this exercise.

AWARE

(10–15 minutes)

Read this section aloud with the students, and draw attention to the ways we numb our bodily sensations. Give students time to journal about their reflections.

ALIVE

(20–30 minutes)

The Aware section leads into a conversation about listening to the signals our bodies give us. The group activity is intended to help students become aware of how much or how little they are in touch with their bodies. Please note that this activity could be difficult or triggering for students. Be aware of any students who have past experiences that might trigger a strong reaction, such as abuse or an eating disorder. Allow them to pace themselves and participate as much or as little as they are able. The following instructions are also included in the student guide: *If one wall of the room you are in represents the statement, "I am in touch with my body, and I listen to what it tells me," and the opposite wall represents the statement, "I never listen to my body," where do you think you are in this range of experiences? Go stand in the place representing your experience.*

Group discussion about this activity will be important to frame and process this activity. Lead this discussion, and help students talk about their experience.

One more activity is offered to help students experience their physical bodies. This activity simply invites students to clench their fists tightly and then unclench them, and then to smile and then relax their faces. Help students notice their bodily sensations.

Another important part of this section is to follow up on the teaching about self-compassion. Read this information to the students, and have them practice a self-soothing exercise. This may feel a little strange to those who are doing this for the first time, but as the leader, you can help to normalize this activity and foster curiosity about trying something new. You may want to give the students time to journal about their experiences with this activity.

ABIDE

(15–20 minutes)

Preparation note: You will be leading the students through a Christian mindfulness practice that is available online. You can stream this from your phone or computer, and the audio track is available on our website: www.theawakenedlife.info.

(10 minutes)

Reiterate the importance of doing the home practices and journaling about it each week. Say the closing blessing in unison together as you close the session.

CONNECTING TO
OTHERS

WORKING THROUGH LONELINESS

PREPARATION FOR THIS SESSION

For this session you will need the following things:

- **Internet access**. You can use the Internet to stream an audio track of Loving-Kindness Meditation 1 in the Awake section and the Great Commandment mindfulness practice in the Abide section. All audio tracks are located at www.theawakenedlife.info.

- **A review of Parker Palmer's Circle of Trust Touchstones**. You may also want to print the Touchstones handout offered on his website at: www.couragerenewal.org/touchstones.

- **Journal and pens**. Students will be asked to journal about certain topics that are covered during this session. This workbook provides some space for journaling; however, students who need more space are invited to bring their own journals. Pens or pencils will also be needed.

(15–20 minutes)

As in previous weeks, take time to first check in regarding the home practices and see how these exercises went for the students. The Awake section then sets the stage to talk about the importance of relationships, and how they impact our well-being. The Awake exercise is a meditation that focuses on extending loving-kindness to those around us. Review the group's covenant once again as a continued invitation for individuals to feel safe within the group.

Preparation note: Once again, the students will be led through a guided meditation. This meditation is available to stream online, or it can be read aloud from the student guide. You can stream the audio track at www.theawakenedlife.info.

Follow this meditation with a closing prayer and a guided conversation.

(5 minutes)

This section teaches students about the prevalence of loneliness and the way it impacts our well-being. Take a moment to read this section aloud as a group.

(30–40 minutes)

In this section, give students a little bit of time to talk about their own experiences with connection and disconnection, drawing from the Aware section. First, lead the full group in a discussion about loneliness, and then break the group into smaller groups of three for the Deep Listening Exercise.

Deep Listening Exercise

Pulling from some of the core components of Parker Palmer's Circle of Trust Touchstones, this exercise allows students the opportunity to be fully present to one another as they share deeply.[25] Emphasize the importance of listening quietly and being present, without fixing. As you may have learned during your Leader's Training Retreat, it might be helpful to revisit the Touchstones again before leading this section.[26] You can find this information online at: www.couragerenewal.org/touchstones. It might even be beneficial to print copies of the Touchstones handout for your group.

Finish this section with a large group conversation about the Deep Listening Exercise. How was this for the students?

(10 minutes)

The Abide exercise is a guided meditation called "The Great Commandment Mindfulness Practice."

Preparation note: This meditation is available to stream online, or it can be read aloud from the student guide. You can stream the audio track at www.theawakenedlife.info

(10 minutes)

Continue to reinforce the weekly practices and encourage students to journal each time they complete them. Together, read the closing blessing.

CONNECTING TO OTHERS

WORKING THROUGH SHAME

PREPARATION FOR THIS SESSION

For this session you will need the following things:

- **Internet access and a screen.** You can use the Internet to stream an audio track of Loving-Kindness Meditation 2 in the Awake section. The Aware section asks students to stream a TEDx video of Brené Brown called "The Power of Vulnerability," which is also available online. You can show this video to the whole group on a large screen or have the students watch the video on their phones in small groups if this is easier. All audio tracks and important links are located at: www.theawakenedlife.info.

- **Journal and pens.** Students will be asked to journal about certain topics that are covered during this session. This workbook provides some space for journaling; however, students who need more space are invited to bring their own journals. Pens or pencils will also be needed.

- **Bread and grape juice for communion.** This session ends by having communion or an interfaith blessing together as a group. Make sure to bring bread and juice to use for the liturgy.

(10–15 minutes)

As in previous weeks, take time to first check in regarding the home practices and see how these exercises went for the students. Read aloud the paragraphs in the Awake section, which begins a conversation about connection and intimacy. The Awake exercise is a meditation expanding on the previous week and focuses on extending loving-kindness to those around us. You can stream the meditation online or read it aloud to the group.

(30–40 minutes)

Preparation note: The TEDx video of Brené Brown is about 20 minutes long. As noted, this will require Internet access and a video screen. In the video, Dr. Brown discusses vulnerability and shame. It might be helpful to watch the video before the session, to understand and be prepared for discussing the content. This may also be a good time to review the Group Covenant made in the first week, to reinforce the guidelines established and build safety in the group.

This video discusses complex emotions. After watching the video, students are asked to reflect personally on what came up for them about shame in their lives. Allow ample time and space for students to reflect on these issues. Please note that this exercise may trigger complex feelings for the students.

Additionally, be aware that this week is full of material, and the video requires a significant chunk of time. You may decide to skip the video and go straight to the journaling exercises if you are pressed for time.

ALIVE

(20–30 minutes)

Read aloud the paragraphs written in the Alive section, under the two Teaching Moment sections. Allow students a little more time to journal about shame triggers on their own, and then bring the group together for either large or small group discussion about shame. This might be a difficult conversation to have for some students, so be sensitive to what is coming up in the group, and allow time and space to process these feelings.

ABIDE

(10–15 minutes)

The conversation about shame and vulnerability will end with a time of communion. Read the communion liturgy as a group. You, as the leader, will read the words in normal text, and the group will read together the words in bold. If you do not identify as Christian or feel uncomfortable leading communion, feel free to use the interfaith blessing at the end of the section as an alternative.

Preparation note: Make sure to have the bread and juice available at this time. Be aware of any food allergies. You may want to provide a gluten-free option.

(10 minutes)

Close with a reminder about completing the weekly home practices, and read the closing blessing together.

CONNECTING TO CREATION

EXPERIENCING AWE OF NATURE

PREPARATION FOR THIS SESSION

For this session you will need the following things:

- **Internet access.** You can use the Internet to stream an audio track of the "Canticle of Brother Sun and Sister Moon" by St. Francis of Assisi in the Awake section. All audio tracks and important links are located at: www.theawakenedlife.info.

- **Plans for a prayer walk**. The mindful walking meditation is intended to take place outside, but if the weather does not permit, students can walk around the room or building. Encourage them to be mindful of their feet touching the ground and the sensations around them even if they are unable to be outside.

- **Journal and pens**. Students will be asked to journal about certain topics that are covered during this session. This workbook provides some space for journaling; however, students who need more space are invited to bring their own journals. Pens or pencils will also be needed.

- **Information regarding the Wesleyan Fast.** Students are asked to engage in a Wesleyan Fast between Week 6 and Week 7. Explain the details of what this fast entails, and let students know that it is OK if they are unable to engage in a food fast. Help them to think of other things to abstain from instead, including television, chocolate, social media, and so forth.
- **Plans for the upcoming meal in Week 7.** Next week you will be cooking and eating a meal together as a group. This week, Week 6, asks the students to do a short fast in preparation for sharing a meal together in Week 7. As you prepare for next week, think about engaging all of the students in this process. It may be beneficial to visit a local farmers market and get produce that is in season to help students make a connection with the earth. You may even want to visit a community garden or nearby farm. Start planning for this process now.

AWAKE

(10–15 minutes)

Listen to the audio track together as a group or read the transcript aloud from the student guide. Instruct your students in how to do centering prayer before they listen to the "Canticle of Brother Sun and Sister Moon" by St. Francis of Assisi. Make sure they each understand to pick a sacred word to return to when their minds begin to wander. Close this section with a time of group discussion. This audio track is available to stream at: www.theawakenedlife.info.

 AWARE

(10–15 minutes)

Read the Aware section out loud and allow the students time to journal about their connection to God through the natural world.

 ALIVE

(30–35 minutes)

In this section, students are encouraged to go on a nature/prayer walk. Allow students about 15 minutes for this. Encourage them to set a timer on their phone to remind them when time is up, but to keep their phones in their bags or pockets during the walk so they can be present to their surroundings. Prepare them to be grateful for what they see, hear, smell, or touch and to really observe nature. They are also asked to choose one living organism (leaf, bug, etc.) to focus on for a few moments. When students return, ask them to engage in group conversation about what they noticed.

 ABIDE

(10 minutes)

This section will involve a brief explanation of fasting and will provide instructions on how to do a fast. Explain this discipline to your students and take time to address any questions that they might have. Keep in mind that some students will not be physically able to complete a food fast, which is fine. You can provide alternative things for them to abstain from instead. You are invited to do this fast together on the same day if this works for your group. This can lead up nicely to the meal that you will cook together next week. However, it is also possible for students to simply do this on their own throughout the week and share about their experience with the larger group.

ARISE

(10 minutes)

Students are asked to continue journaling and doing their mindfulness meditations, and to also incorporate their fasts this week. There are several helpful questions in the Abide section that the students are asked to reflect on in their home practices. Make sure to point this out and make sure they are prepared.

Preparation note: Meal prep—Ideally, the group leader will lead students in preparing a meal together next week, which is Week 7. Of course, this may not be possible given each unique ministry setting. For those who are able, assign students to prepare different dishes or bring in various ingredients. Simple ideas for meals that are collaborative in terms of individual ingredients are tacos (lettuce, tomatoes, cheese, tortillas, etc.) or pizza (crust, sauce, cheese, toppings, etc.). If cooking a meal together is not possible, a potluck option would also be a good idea for this week. It is also totally acceptable to order something in. Start this conversation at the end of Week 6, so you are prepared and have a plan in place for next week's activities.

Read the closing blessing together in unison.

CONNECTING TO CREATION

PREPARATION FOR THIS SESSION

For this session you will need:

- **Meal prep plan**. As a reminder from last week, the group leader will lead students in preparing a meal together this week. Based upon the meal you chose, we simply ask you to be mindful of the meal together and follow the steps in the student guide to facilitate conversation and mindful awareness of how the table brings us together.

- **Knowledge of what ingredients will be used in the meal**. Students will do a little bit of Internet research on what it takes to grow, cultivate, or create each item that they will eat today. In small groups, they will research cheese, tomatoes, or bread, as examples. Think ahead about which ingredients you want them to focus on in small groups.

- **Internet access**. Students will use the Internet on their phones to do a little research about the ingredients in the meal you eat together.

- **Journal and pens**. Students will be asked to journal about certain topics covered during this session. This workbook provides some space for journaling; however, students who need more space are invited to bring their own journals. Pens or pencils will also be needed.

(5–10 minutes)

Open by checking in regarding the home practices, and specifically about the fast. Have some group conversation about how this went for each student. How has their relationship to food (or whatever they abstained from) changed? Read the Awake section aloud as a group. Begin thinking about your relationship with food, and cultivate gratitude for this gift you have been given.

(15–20 minutes)

After reading this section aloud, divide students into small groups based on the various ingredients in your meal. Have them write down what they find out about how this ingredient is likely grown, cultivated, or made. Have them note any issues of social justice in consuming or shipping this item and note any nutritional information about the ingredient that might be interesting. Have a large group conversation about what each group finds.

ALIVE

(60–75 minutes)

Prepare and eat your meal together. Intentionally talk about the process of washing, chopping, cooking, and eating. We ask you try to spend the first ten minutes of the meal in silence, in order to focus on the sensations associated with eating. Then have group conversation about what this process was like.

ABIDE

(10–15 minutes)

The Ignatian method of prayer is taught in this section. It is possible that your group will not have time to complete this if you are preparing and eating a meal from scratch. Feel free to assign this for home practices between sessions. If your group ordered food in and/or has more time, feel free to walk through the steps of this method of prayer as a closing prayer after your meal together.

ARISE

(5 minutes)

Remind students that their home practices continue. Also, next week will be your last session together. You may want to prep students for the closing of their time together and talk about any feelings they might be having as the end of their time together draws near. Say the closing blessing together as you end your meal and time together.

CLOSING

AWAKENING TO JOY

PREPARATION FOR THIS SESSION

For this session you will need the following things:

- **Internet access**. You can use the Internet to stream an audio track of the Gratitude Meditation in the Awake section. All audio tracks and important links are located at www.theawakenedlife.info.

- **Large Post-it Notes, a chalkboard, or a whiteboard and markers**. During the Aware segment, your group will be asked to brainstorm about their takeaways from your eight weeks together. It would be helpful to pre-label seven Post-it Notes, each with the title of one of the seven weeks, and have students reflect on what they gleaned from them.

- **Journal and pens**. Students will be asked to journal about certain topics during the gratitude exercise in this session. This workbook provides some space for journaling; however, students who need more space are invited to bring their own journals. Pens or pencils will also be needed.

- **Letter-writing materials (blank paper, envelopes, and pens).** Students will be asked to write a letter to themselves regarding this journey, which you will collect and hand back to them next semester.
- **Token of course completion.** Often, to symbolize the ending of an important event, a small token is given to each participant to carry with them. This is completely optional but might be meaningful. Ideas for this token include bookmarks, small stones with inspirational words on them, or printed photos of the group. Feel free to make this symbol personal and unique.

AWAKE

(5–10 minutes)

Once again, check in regarding the home practices. Remind students that even though the group is ending, these are practices they can carry with them forever. After reading the Awake section paragraphs as a group, do the Gratitude Meditation together. You can either listen to the audio track online or read the transcript aloud from the student guide. After the meditation, spend some time reflecting on how the students have experienced these meditation practices over the course of the eight weeks.

AWARE

(10–20 minutes)

During the Aware segment, students will reflect and brainstorm about their most powerful insights from each week.

Preparation note: Use large Post-it Notes or a whiteboard. Make sure to have markers or pens, and allow the students to brainstorm freely.

(30–40 minutes)

The group gratitude exercise can be a powerful opportunity to reflect on the connections made between group members and express the value of each person in the group. Depending on the size of your group, this may take a little bit of time. Allow three minutes per pairing, and then give the students some time to reflect individually on what they heard from one another.

Drawing from this experience, have students write a letter to themselves about insights they have learned and ways they have grown over the course of these eight weeks.

Preparation note: This is the time to use the letter-writing materials. Make sure each student labels the outside of their envelope with their full name so you can return the letters to each student next semester. If the students are graduating or moving on from the university, feel free to have them self-address the envelope and send the letters to their home address. It might even be easier to mail everyone's letters to their home addresses if postage is not an issue for you.

(10–15 minutes)

Walk students through the Daily Examen as a closing meditation practice.

ARISE

(10–15 minutes)

As you prepare to leave from the group, remind participants of the importance of ongoing practice even after the group is over. They will continue to have access to the website and are free to use the recorded meditations at any point.

As you end, recognize that endings can bring up all kinds of emotions. Allow students to be present with what they may be feeling—accomplishment, gratitude, sadness, or even relief.

Preparation note: At this point, if you have chosen to give a token to the participants to symbolize the end of your time together, hand this out now and explain the significance of your item.

Close together by saying the closing blessing in unison.

NOTES

1 Steve Bradt, "Wandering Mind Not a Happy Mind," *Harvard Gazette*, November 11, 2010, https://news.harvard.edu/gazette/story/2010/11/wandering-mind-not -a-happy-mind/.

2 Bob Stahl and Elisha Goldstein, *A Mindfulness-Based Stress Reduction Workbook* (Oakland: New Harbinger Publications, 2010), 55–56.

3 Kristin Neff, *Self-Compassion: The Proven Power of Being Kind to Yourself* (New York: HarperCollins, 2011), 39–106.

4 Amy Oden, *Right Here Right Now: The Practice of Christian Mindfulness* (Nashville: Abingdon, 2011), 57.

5 John Wesley, "The Character of a Methodist," in Wesley, *The Works of the Reverend John Wesley, A.M.* (New York: T. Mason and G. Lane, 1839), 5:242.

6 Adapted from Amy Oden, *Right Here Right Now, The Practice of Christian Mindfulness* (Nashville: Abingdon Press, 2011), 57.

7 Adapted from Mark Williams and Danny Penman, *Mindfulness: An Eight-Week Plan for Finding Peace in a Frantic World* (New York: Rodale Books, 2012), 73–75.

8 Deborah J. Cohan, "Cell Phones and College Students," *Psychology Today*, April 30, 2016, https://www.psychologytoday.com/us/blog/social-lights/201604/cell -phones-and-college-students.

9 Mayo Clinic staff, "Stress Symptoms: Effects on your Body and Behavior," Mayo Clinic, April 28, 2016, https://www.mayoclinic.org/healthy-lifestyle/stress -management/in-depth/stress-symptoms/art-20050987.

10 Tara Brach, *True Refuge: Finding Peace and Freedom in Your Own Awakened Heart* (New York: Random House, 2012), 26.

11 CBS News, "Many Americans Are Lonely, and Gen Z Most of All, Study Finds," May 3, 2018, https://www.cbsnews.com/news/many-americans-are-lonely -and-gen-z-most-of-all-study-finds/.

12 Anna Haensch, "When Choirs Sing, Many Hearts Beat as One," NPR, July 10, 2013, https://www.npr.org/sections/health-shots/2013/07/09/200390454/when -choirs-sing-many-hearts-beat-as-one.

13 Brené Brown, *Daring Greatly: How the Courage to Be Vulnerable Transforms the Way We Live, Love, Parent, and Lead* (New York: Penguin Random House, 2012), 71.

14 Brené Brown, *I Thought It Was Just Me (but It Isn't): Telling the Truth about Perfectionism, Inadequacy and Power* (New York: Penguin Random House, 2007), Companion Worksheet, retrieved from https://brenebrown.com/wp-content /uploads/2013/09/ITIWJMreadingguide.pdf.

15 Brené Brown, "Listening to Shame," TED video, presented to a local audience at TEDxHouston, June 2010, https://www.ted.com/talks/brene_brown_listening _to_shame/transcript?language=en#t-67083.

16 Modified from a Service of Word and Table II, *United Methodist Hymnal*, 13–15, and *United Methodist Hymnal*, 15–16.

17 Howard Frumkin et al., "Nature Contact and Human Health: A Research Agenda," Environmental Health Perspectives 125, no. 7 (July 2017), https://ehp.niehs.nih .gov/doi/10.1289/EHP1663.

18 Nielsen Media, "The Nielsen Total Audience Report: Q1 2016," 4, available for download at Nielsen.com, http://www.nielsen.com/us/en/insights/reports /2016/the-total-audience-report-q1-2016.html.

19 Frumkin et al., "Nature Contact and Human Health."

20 Steve Manskar, "Fasting, the Most Neglected Means of Grace," *Equipping Disciples: A Discipleship Ministries Blog*, February 18, 2015, https://blog.umc discipleship.org/fasting-the-most-neglected-means-of-grace/.

21 Lily Rose, "1 in 3 Americans Can't Eat a Meal Without Being on Their Phone," *Orlando Sentinel*, January 24, 2018, http://www.orlandosentinel.com/features/food

/sns-dailymeal-1867994-eat-americans-cant-eat-without-being-on-their-phones
-20180124-story.html.

22 Upper Room Ministries, "The Ignatian Method of Prayer," The Upper Room
https://www.upperroom.org/resources/the-ignatian-method-of-prayer.

23 Adapted from Loyola Press, "How Can I Pray?" IgnatianSpirituality.com, accessed January 14, 2019, https://www.ignatianspirituality.com/ignatian-prayer
/the-examen/how-can-i-pray.

24 Amy G. Oden, *Right Here Right Now: The Practice of Christian Mindfulness*
(Nashville: Abingdon Press, 2011).

25 Parker Palmer, *A Hidden Wholeness: The Journey Toward an Undivided Life*
(San Francisco: Jossey-Bass, 2004).

26 Parker Palmer, *Let Your Life Speak: Listening for the Voice of Vocation* (San Francisco: Jossey-Bass, 2000).

ACKNOWLEDGMENTS

We would like to extend a special thank-you to our working group members who brainstormed alongside us and supported this work from the beginning: Timothy Eberhart, Victoria Hart Gaskell, Soomee Kim, Bryan Langlands, Meg Lassiat, Amy Oden, Karen Oliveto, Megan Otto, and Jasper Peters. Thank you for your grace and insight. Thank you to our pilot site leaders, who were willing and able to try new things, give feedback, and engage in this process with us: Laura Kirkpatrick, Tonya Lawrence, Ian McDonald, Megan Otto, Stacey Shanks, and Keith Turner. We are immensely grateful for the wisdom and hospitality of Judy Skeen, who provided space and guidance for us to teach these practices.

9 781945 935497